WHAT EFFECTIVE SCHOOLS DO

Re-Envisioning the Correlates

LAWRENCE W. LEZOTTE
KATHLEEN McKEE SNYDER

Solution Tree | Press

a division of
Solution Tree

555 North Morton Street
Bloomington, IN 47404
800.733.6786 (toll free) / 812.336.7700
FAX: 812.336.7790

email: info@solution-tree.com
solution-tree.com

Printed in the United States of America

14 13 12 11   3 4 5

FSC
Mixed Sources
Product group from well-managed
forests and other controlled sources

Cert no. SW-COC-002283
www.fsc.org
© 1996 Forest Stewardship Council

Library of Congress Cataloging-in-Publication Data

Lezotte, Lawrence W.
    What effective schools do : re-envisioning the correlates / Lawrence W. Lezotte, Kathleen McKee Snyder.
        p. cm.
    Includes bibliographical references.
    ISBN 978-1-935249-51-1 (softbound) -- ISBN 978-1-935249-52-8 (library binding) 1. School improvement programs--United States. 2. Teacher effectiveness--United States. 3. Curriculum planning--United States. 4. Educational leadership--United States. 5. Lesson planning--United States. I. Snyder, Kathleen McKee. II. Title.
    LB1025.3.L496 2011
    371.2'07--dc22
                                                                    2010027602

Solution Tree
Jeffrey C. Jones, CEO & President

Solution Tree Press
President: Douglas M. Rife
Publisher: Robert D. Clouse
Vice President of Production: Gretchen Knapp
Managing Production Editor: Caroline Wise
Proofreader: Rachel Rosolina
Text Designer: Raven Bongiani

Cover Designer: Pam Rude

Acknowledgments

Books don't write themselves, and authors are rarely solely responsible for the content of their books. We are no different.

We want to acknowledge the efforts of so many educators and researchers who believed in the idea that all children could learn and worked diligently to find those schools that were successful at doing so. We especially want to acknowledge those whose research we reference in this book. Each study selected provided the foundational evidence of the correlate or a clear example of the correlate in practice.

We also want to acknowledge the educators who have helped us in the past and continue to help us bring research to practitioners by translating research articles into everyday language for the Effective Schools Research Abstracts, the forerunner to Research LiNK™, an online archive containing abstracts of school improvement research accessible through the effective schools website (www .effectiveschools.com). These experienced and insightful educators continue to make invaluable contributions to our research-based resources. We would also like to acknowledge the indispensable Effective Schools staff—Kate, Paula, and Becky—who keep all the balls in the air while we're off writing, and who provide invaluable input into all aspects of the business. And no acknowledgment would be complete without mentioning Ruth, who keeps us all on our toes.

Finally, we extend our thanks to the many educators who participated in our surveys and offered us—and you—the benefit of their experiences and insights. We hope that this blend of research and the voices from practice will add to the richness of the school reform conversation, as well as provide a powerful system of support for educators as they seek to improve student learning for all children.

Lawrence W. Lezotte

Kathleen McKee Snyder

Solution Tree Press would like to thank the following reviewers:

Janet Chrispeels
Professor, Department of Education Studies
University of California San Diego
San Diego, California

Anthony C. Frontier
Assistant Professor, Education Department
Cardinal Stritch University
Milwaukee, Wisconsin

William Owings
Professor, Department of Educational Foundations and Leadership
Editor, *Journal of Effective Schools*
Old Dominion University
Norfolk, Virginia

Table of Contents

Part II
The Correlates of Effective Schools Defined . . . 37

Chapter 6

Opportunity to Learn/Time on Task 75

Chapter 7

Frequent Monitoring of Student Progress 91

Chapter 8

Safe and Orderly Environment 101

Part III
Putting the Correlates to Work in an Effective Learning System 129

About the Authors

Dr. Lawrence W. Lezotte earned his doctorate from Michigan State University (MSU) in 1969, joining the faculty there that same year. During his eighteen-year tenure at MSU, he served in various capacities, including chair of the Department of Educational Administration; associate director, with Ron Edmonds, of the Center for School Improvement in the College of Education; and chair of Urban and Metropolitan Studies in the College of Urban Affairs. Dr. Lezotte was a member of the original team of effective schools researchers who identified the characteristics of successful schools that have come to be known as the correlates of effective schools.

Since that time, Dr. Lezotte has been at the forefront of the effective schools movement and has written widely on the new mission of public education. He has identified the components of a learner-centered system, as well as the theories and tools necessary for successful and continuous school improvement.

As a nationally renowned education consultant and speaker, Dr. Lezotte has devoted his career to assisting schools in their efforts to ensure that all students learn. He touches the lives of thousands of educators and tens of thousands of students each year through training programs, workshops, and conferences across the United States and Canada. Dr. Lezotte's training programs not only inspire schools and districts to adopt the learning-for-all mission, but also give them the information and tools they need to plan and implement continuous school improvement and raise student achievement. In recognition of his lifelong efforts, Dr. Lezotte received the 2003 Council of Chief State School Officers' Distinguished Service Award presented each year to an outstanding American who has made a difference in education. Dr. Lezotte was also selected as the 2009 recipient of the prestigious Brock International Prize in Education. The award is given annually to recognize an individual for innovative and effective ideas in education resulting in a significant impact on the practice or understanding of the field of education.

Kathleen McKee Snyder earned her master's degree in 1980 from Michigan State University in Community and Regional Development within the College of Agriculture and Natural Resources. The primary focus of her work there was in the area of community and organizational change, and the role of leadership in creating stakeholder buy-in and consensus. During her time at MSU, she coordinated the Lansing Community Network, a diverse group of citizens who, under the College of Urban Affairs, worked together to bring about positive changes in their community, particularly in regard to the education and welfare of young people. Ms. Snyder also consulted with various communities and nonprofit organizations in conducting perceptual surveys of their stakeholder groups and assisting them in creating buy-in to their various improvement efforts.

In 1987, Ms. Snyder became the executive director of an environmental education center in mid-Michigan, where she became well acquainted with the public education system. Working closely with local school districts, Ms. Snyder facilitated the alignment of the center's K–8 education programs with state learning objectives in core areas. During her ten years at the center, she instituted several hands-on science and environmental education programs designed to augment the curricula of the local schools. Ms. Snyder also has firsthand experience with education through her experiences as a substitute teacher in elementary and middle schools, and with her involvement as a parent of three children. Her varied experiences with public education, combined with her knowledge of the change process, continuous improvement, and leadership, have allowed Ms. Snyder to bring a unique perspective to her work at Effective Schools.

Ms. Snyder joined Effective Schools Products in 2000 as editor of the Effective Schools Research Abstracts. She continues to edit school improvement research abstracts for the online Effective Schools Research LiNK and has coauthored three other books with Dr. Lezotte: *Assembly Required: A Continuous School Improvement System* (2002), its companion *Implementation Guide* (2004), and *Stepping Up: Leading the Charge to Improve Our Schools* (2006).

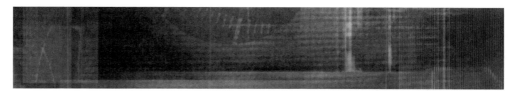

Introduction

What is an effective school? What factors characterize an effective school? What needs to happen to make a school effective? These questions are central to the effective schools research. This research was launched in response to a conclusion of the Equal Educational Opportunity (EEO) Study (Coleman, 1966). According to this study, family background—not the school—was the major determinant of student achievement. This conclusion prompted a vigorous reaction leading to many studies that would later come to define the research base for the effective schools movement. The educational researchers who conducted these studies developed a body of research that supported the premise that all children can learn and that the school controls the factors necessary to ensure student mastery of the core curriculum. Of course, the effective schools researchers did not discount the important impact of the family on student learning. Ron Edmonds, one of the original effective schools researchers, observed that "while schools may be primarily responsible for whether or not students function adequately in school, the family is probably critical in determining whether or not students flourish in school" (1982, p. 4).

Findings from effective schools research have provided schools and districts with a vast resource and solid foundation for today's school improvement efforts. This large body of research has yielded a set of seven characteristics that successful schools share—schools that successfully teach all children regardless of socioeconomic status or ethnicity. These characteristics have come to be known as the correlates of effective schools. The correlates of effective schools have evolved through two generations; the first generation was the minimum standard the school needed to attain to be considered effective. As the body of research grew, our understanding of each correlate deepened, and the second generation of correlates emerged. The second generation takes the correlates one step further, expanding them in important ways that further the learning-for-all mission. The correlates of effective schools are now defined as follows:

- High expectations for success
- Strong instructional leadership
- Clear and focused mission
- Opportunity to learn/time on task
- Frequent monitoring of student progress

- Safe and orderly environment
- Positive home-school relations

Re-Envisioning the Correlates of Effective Schools

Effective Schools Products has previously published a series of books that highlight the research and proven practices associated with each correlate (Lezotte & McKee, 2002, 2004, 2006). Many schools and districts have used these books to enable their teams to access the research around each correlate. In this book, we build upon the previous works by expanding the discussion around each correlate, updating the knowledge base, and incorporating practical ideas from practitioners in the field. In re-envisioning the correlates for effective schools, we provide further clarification about the factors that characterize an effective school and what educators can do to ensure that their schools exemplify the correlates. We continue our tradition of emphasizing foundational research studies from the past and adding observations from recent contemporary research. We hope that these examples will illustrate that even though effective schools research has been around for decades, it continues to evolve, expand, and become even more useful in school reform efforts. Most of the studies we cite can be accessed at the Effective Schools Research LiNK, an online database containing abstracts of school improvement research (see appendix B, page 145, for details). The Research LiNK is updated regularly throughout the school year.

Practitioner Perspectives and Insights

We believe that education has generally done an inadequate job of capturing and sharing the wisdom of successful practitioners with other educators. In an effort to remedy this shortcoming and to learn about the perspectives and insights of practitioners at both school and district levels, we have used Reality Check™, a series of online surveys (see appendix B for details). These surveys, based on each correlate, invited thousands of educators to share their views of the correlate, noting problems and issues associated with each, and to describe practices that have worked for them in addressing these factors. The educators who responded to these surveys had relationships with Effective Schools Products through training, Larry Lezotte's consulting, and the Superintendency Institute, as well as others who have purchased our products or signed up to receive our mailings. In each correlate chapter, we tell how many educators responded to the survey and describe the demographic according to percentage of teachers or principals at elementary, middle, and secondary school levels, as well as the percentage of respondents who identified themselves from the central office. These surveys were not meant to provide scientific data, but were intended to illustrate a sampling of how practitioners viewed the correlates and their suggestions for using them. The practitioner views and suggestions came from hundreds of educators who cared enough to take time from their busy schedules to share their thoughts with us. We found their input valuable and sensible, and we think you will, too. We incorporate their input into the "Correlate in Action" section of chapters 3 through 9. The information obtained from these surveys provides insight into what needs to happen to make a school effective.

Using the Correlates

The correlates of effective schools can be considered in two ways. First, they can be viewed as a set of interdependent components that define the complex infrastructure of a school. This perspective offers a basis on which to compare schools and determine why some are effective and others are not. To use the correlates in this fashion means that a school must be prepared to address all seven correlates at once.

Second, for purposes of a deeper understanding of planned school change, we can examine each correlate individually. This approach may seem antithetical to the first perspective, but it's really not. Consider this analogy: we could study a modern automobile in its entirety as a complex system of interdependent parts. We could also learn about the car by studying separately each of the major components that contribute to its overall performance. To keep the car running at peak performance, we need to be able to diagnose and repair each part, but we also need to make sure all the parts are working together properly. Similarly, learning about what constitutes an effective school requires knowledge of the individual correlates and the interrelationships among them.

As we look anew at the correlates of effective schools, we strive to maintain a balance between these two perspectives. Throughout the book, we will continually remind you of the interdependent nature of the overall network of components that defines the effective school as a system; we will do this as we describe each correlate at the conceptual level as well as at the operational level. In this way, we provide resources for educators to measure and monitor the use of each correlate in their schools in a practical and efficient manner. We also examine the research associated with each correlate and interpret that research in a way that makes sense in the classroom and the school. After all, our purpose is to describe not only what effective schools are, but also what they do.

Developing a Data Dashboard

Monitoring progress in the application of the correlates is an essential feature of successful school improvement efforts. We describe a framework for using the correlates as the leading indicators of learning. These indicators are the focal points for creating a data dashboard, which provides information about implementation of the correlate. The data can be obtained from perceptual surveys, stakeholder self reports, and third-party direct observations. As you read about each correlate, we encourage you to develop a data dashboard, selecting specific measures for that correlate that you believe best fit your context. Ideally, by the end of each correlate chapter, you'll have chosen measures that you can use initially to assess and subsequently monitor change as you plan and implement each correlate. Remember, the indicators you choose should be tailored to your school or district.

Perceptual Surveys

Perceptual surveys are used to assess the presence or absence and strength or weakness of the correlates in a school setting. The rationale for using such surveys is based on two important principles. First, there is the old sociological axiom that if something is perceived as real, it is real in its consequences. For example, if parents perceive the school to be unsafe, or if teachers perceive that they don't have enough time to teach the curriculum, or if students perceive that the teachers do not care about them, these perceptions can become the reality for the individuals. These perceptions have the potential to become self-fulfilling prophecies. Knowing about the perceptions of individuals involved in the school improvement effort is enlightening for leaders who are responsible for bringing about change. Second, perceptual surveys are efficient in that they can be administered and analyzed quickly and inexpensively.

One major shortcoming of perceptual surveys is that the validity of the data depends on the willingness of respondents to be honest, rather than to simply provide what they perceive to be the desired response. Staff members and other stakeholders are more likely to give honest responses if they can be assured of anonymity, and that the survey data will only be used to improve the school. Another limitation of perceptual surveys stems from the structure of the question responses, which typically invite respondents to react to a given scale (for example, strongly agree to strongly disagree). As a result, perceptual surveys are generally limited in the depth of information that can be gathered. Nonetheless, this type of survey allows respondents to answer many questions quickly, which prompts a higher response rate and a more complete overall picture of the perceptions.

Surveying stakeholders is critical to the school improvement process not only because it provides key information, but also because involving them builds commitment to the process. Surveying can be very time consuming, however. For that reason, we recommend that school leaders take advantage of online resources to create, administer, and analyze surveys. The examples of perceptual survey items we present in the correlate chapters are drawn from Reality Check, an online survey tool from Effective Schools Products.

Stakeholder Self Reports

Like perceptual surveys, self-reporting instruments can be designed for any stakeholder group (such as parents, teachers, students, and other members of the school community). Self-report systems differ from surveys in that the participants are asked to construct or reconstruct a response from memory, or from actual data (rather than from opinion). For example, a student might be asked how many times his teacher called on him last week. Parents might be asked to indicate how many times they initiated a phone conversation with a teacher during the current school year. Teachers might be asked to indicate how many disciplinary-based classroom interruptions they experienced during the previous week.

Self reports may also ask the respondents to develop a more detailed narrative response to a question. For example, teachers might be asked to indicate how they would respond to a critical emergency or some problem in the classroom. Self-report questions allow for some exploration of the emotional aspects of the situation—teachers might be asked to describe how they feel about the new discipline policy in the school. The possibilities are unlimited, but the investigator must be cautious: the more demands placed on respondents, the lower the response rate will be. Likewise, the more questions the respondent is asked, the more likely fatigue will begin to influence the thoughtfulness and thoroughness of the responses.

Generally speaking, we have found that educationally related stakeholders are willing to provide responses even if it requires some work on their part (up to a point). Self reports provide a rich and textured picture of current reality as seen through the eyes of the individual stakeholder, but one must balance the desire for answers with the time and energy it takes to provide them.

The analysis of the more subjective self-report information places a burden on the shoulders of the data analyst. To analyze open-ended responses, a set of categories is needed with each response assigned to only one category. While this task can be laborious if the number of respondents is large, the self-report tool does allow you to create a profile of the respondent population.

Third-Party Direct Observations

Like perceptual surveys and self reports, third-party direct observation techniques have certain advantages and limitations. For some of the correlates, it is difficult to get accurate data through perceptual surveys or self reports. For example, when asked to indicate student engagement rates during a literacy lesson, teachers tend to have difficulty responding to the question simply because they are preoccupied with teaching the lesson. It is very hard for one person to be both the conductor of the orchestra and the critic at the same time.

In contrast, placing a third party in the classroom who has been trained to scan the class during the lesson and make specific recordings regarding student engagement will yield more reliable data. If the same observer collects the same data from several classrooms, the data are more likely to be stable since the same rules of engagement are being used across all the observations.

Cost is the major limitation of third-party direct observation techniques. Placing an observer in each classroom long enough to capture an accurate picture of the operations takes time, and time is money. However, if a school or district has the opportunity and resources to collect information regarding the correlates using a third party, we encourage them to do so.

In constructing the school's data dashboard, we recommend using a combination of the three tools described. Some information can be gathered quickly and reliably using perceptual surveys or self reports, while other information requires direct observation and more deliberation. An accurate profile of a school usually incorporates information from a variety of sources and a range of topics, including such factors as academic performance, student demographics, professional learning experiences, and finances.

Features of This Book

What Effective Schools Do is designed as guide to assist educators with activities for implementing a continuous school improvement system through application of the seven correlates of effective schools. The ten chapters provide a comprehensive description of practices that enable educators to build and sustain a school culture that accommodates the learning expectations and needs of all students. This book is organized in three parts:

- Part I—The Correlates of Effective Schools in Context (chapters 1 and 2) describes the historical context in which the correlates have evolved, examines the school as a system, and provides perspectives on systems changes.

- Part II—The Correlates of Effective Schools Defined (chapters 3 through 9) explores the individual correlates and provides research-based resources for examining and implementing each one.

- Part III—Putting the Correlates to Work in an Effective Learning System (chapter 10) explains how the correlates are used to establish a continuous school improvement system.

Several features facilitate the use of resources in this book.

- Definitions of Key Terms—Chapter 1 provides definitions of terms associated with effective schools research. The chapters in part II open with a definition of the correlate that is the topic of that chapter.

- Tools for Monitoring Change—Perceptual surveys, stakeholder self reports, and third-party direct observations are three tools described in the context of each correlate featured in the chapters in part II. Examples of these tools, provided at the end of each chapter, are intended to help educators create a data dashboard through which to monitor progress on implementing the correlates.

- Practitioner Perspectives and Insights—This section of the correlates chapters (part II) presents examples of responses to Reality Check online surveys. These examples provide insight into what happens when educators are involved in applying the correlates in their schools or districts.

- Research-Supported Strategies—This section of the correlates chapters (part II) summarizes results from studies that have investigated school improvement and reform efforts.

- Appendices—The appendices include a list foundational research readings and descriptions of selected resources from Effective Schools Products, including Research LiNK and Reality Check surveys.

This book will be useful to a variety of audiences. If you are familiar with the correlates of effective schools, we think you'll find this updated look at the correlates helpful in taking the conversation one step further as it brings together theory, research, and practitioners' perspectives. Administrators will find the book useful in explaining the correlates to their colleagues and staff. New or aspiring teachers will find a strong foundation for their future in teaching.

Some might think that effective schools research is old news because it has been around a long time. But the simple fact is, when the correlates and the effective schools process are applied with fidelity and commitment, they work. Case studies conducted since 1966 have shown that.

Ron Edmonds once said, "We can, whenever and wherever we choose, successfully teach all children whose schooling is of interest to us. We already know more than we need to do that. Whether or not we do it must finally depend on how we feel about the fact that we haven't so far" (1979, p. 20). The correlates of effective schools represent the knowledge educators need to successfully teach all children. Taken together, the correlates are more than just theory; they are what effective schools *do*. We hope you will use them to become more effective as you work toward fulfilling the learning-for-all mission.

PART I

The Correlates of Effective Schools in Context

CHAPTER 1

Evolution of the Effective Schools Concept

The effective school is characterized by high overall student achievement with no significant gaps in that achievement across the major subgroups in the student population. The effective school is built on a foundation of high expectations, strong leadership, unwavering commitment to learning for all, collaboration, differentiated instruction, and frequent monitoring of student progress.

A Short History of Public Education in the United States

Understanding the historical sociocultural context of public education provides insight into issues schools have faced in the past—and continue to encounter today—even though profound changes have occurred in society. Why? If we ignore the path that public education has taken to get to where we are today, we'd be left with an incomplete view of today's schools and the issues they face.

The effective schools concept has evolved since initial research efforts began in the late 1960s, but its underlying philosophy and core values date back to the beginning of the public education system in the United States. In the late 1700s, education throughout the world was primarily a privilege of the wealthy. The founding fathers of the United States believed that the survival of the new democracy depended upon an educated citizenry. Perhaps Thomas Jefferson put it best: "I know no safe depository of the ultimate powers of the society, but the people themselves; and if we think them not enlightened enough to exercise their control with a wholesome discretion, the remedy is not to take it from them, but to inform their discretion by education. This is the true corrective of abuses of constitutional power" (Jefferson, 1899, p. 161). From the earliest days, the debate focused on how best to ensure that all citizens would have access and opportunity to an education that would prepare them for the world in which they would live, work, and vote. This debate continues today, in a changing world with changing needs for students and educators alike.

Educational historian Lawrence Cremin, in his book *Public Education*, framed the historical context from which the effective schools concept has evolved and highlighted how the educational mission has changed:

> For most of human history, men and women have believed that only an elite is worthy and capable of education and that the great mass of people should be trained as hewers of wood and drawers of water, if they were to be trained at all. It was only at the end of the eighteenth century and the beginning of the nineteenth that popular leaders in Europe and America— the Marquis de Condorcet in France, Thomas Jefferson in the United States, and Lord Brougham in England—began to dream of universal school systems that would give everyone a chance to partake of the arts and sciences. Not surprisingly, they had their most immediate successes with the children who were the easiest to teach—those who, through early nurture in the family and other institutions, had been prepared for whatever it was that the schools had to offer.
>
> Now, in the twentieth century, we have turned to the more difficult task, the education of those at the margin—those who suffer from physical, mental and emotional handicaps, those who have long been held at a distance by political or social means, and those who for a variety of other reasons are less ready for what the school has to offer and hence more difficult to teach. (Cremin, 1976, pp. 85–86)

Cremin's statements make it clear how the mission of public education has steadily evolved from education for *some* to education for *all*.

As we retrace the path of public education, we can see this evolution by focusing on how various factors have changed over time. The first factor is *who* is served by the public education system; universal public education for young children is only a little over a century old and continues to be the focus of debate. Universal access for high school students has an even shorter history. Furthermore, the system has not always provided for the educational needs of minorities, those with physical or mental challenges, and young adults beyond the age of compulsory attendance. Today, public education embraces a far broader audience, including the groups mentioned above.

The second factor is the evolution of the core purpose of public schooling. Initially, the primary purpose was to teach the basic knowledge and skills necessary to ensure an understanding of democracy and democratic values. That knowledge and skill set centered on being able to read, perform basic arithmetic, and understand the subjects of history and government to a degree that enabled citizens to understand and make reasoned decisions in elections. As a result of policy changes such as those reflected in No Child Left Behind (2001), the goal of public education has become to remove the major consequences of being economically disadvantaged in America. This shift in purpose represents a profound change in the work of the schools. The observations that Robert Hutchins made in 1956 have as much relevance today as they did over five decades ago. At that time, he summarized the challenge educational leaders must confront in their efforts to promote sustainable school reform:

> Perhaps the greatest idea that America has given the world is the idea of education for all. We have virtually all students going to school. The question before us is: can we truly educate more and more of the students while at the same time taking the curriculum to higher and higher levels? (Hutchins, 1956, p. 29)

How we measure student success in public schools is another significant factor in the evolution of public education. For much of the last century, as public schools focused on ensuring access to the schools, the success of public education was judged by the number of inputs into the system (books, programs, or teachers) and student participation in the school and its programs. For example, regional accreditation programs required schools to report on how many books were in the school library. The accreditation program never asked whether anybody read the books! Likewise, in the early days of the U.S. Office of Education's school recognition program, schools were celebrated because of their fine arts or technology programs. As important as these and other programs are, the programs themselves did not address the consequences for the students.

Today, schools are being judged almost exclusively on the outcomes or results of student achievement, a departure from past practice. Given this change in the approach to public education, any attempt to analyze and evaluate public education at-large or even an individual public school must rest on the achievement of all students. Judging schools by measures that look at the average, mean, or other measure of central tendency clouds the inclusive learning-for-all mission. Disaggregation of student performance data—a concept that originated with effective schools researchers decades ago—is now an accepted process for measuring school success. Effective schools researchers have found disaggregation to be the best available tool to answer the fundamental question: who is profiting, and by how much, from what the schools are currently doing?

The Sameness Standard Under Siege

The early history of public education parallels the history of industrialization in the United States. This coincidence in both time and place has meant that the industrial or factory model has had a significant influence on the organizational structure and culture of the schools. According to Linda Darling-Hammond (1995):

> Today's schools were designed when the goal of education was not to educate all students well, but to process a great many efficiently, selecting and supporting only a few for "thinking work." Strategies for sorting

and tracking students were developed to ration the scarce resources of expert teachers and rich curricula, and to standardize teaching tasks and procedures within groups. (p. 53)

As the idea of the common school became more widespread, the curriculum became more formal and standardized, the one-room schoolhouse was abolished, students were sorted based on age into separate classrooms, and the standard of sameness became the norm. Decades later, factory influences still remain.

Structuring schools in the image of the factory model wherein students are placed in age-based groups would work if the range of individual differences among students the same age were nonexistent or minimal. While student populations were never really homogeneous, the past two decades of unprecedented growth in student diversity, plus an ever-widening economic gap among students have yielded even larger and increasing academic and cultural differences among students. No longer can the problem of individual differences be ignored. The accountability and standards movement has forced educators and policymakers to confront this issue of diversity in the school population.

"The most unequal thing you can do is to treat unequal people equally" is an adage that has particular relevance for school reform efforts designed to meet the learning-for-all mission. Acknowledging differences among students of the same age demands that the "sameness" standard be abandoned. Human learning research has verified that prior knowledge, readiness, and prerequisite skills are strongly predictive of success with new learning (Bodovski & Farkas, 2007; Kainz & Vernon-Feagans, 2007). The fact that some students come to school without having already acquired some of the essential prior knowledge doesn't mean that they *can't* learn. Rather, it should be interpreted to mean that these students haven't yet had the experiences to acquire that knowledge. Logically, this circumstance indicates that each child's education should begin at that child's starting point. To do otherwise is to ensure that children who start with a knowledge deficit will likely be playing catch up throughout their entire school experience. Sadly, this is the experience of far too many children in the public education system.

What are educators to do as they face the challenge of addressing individual differences in a school system structured on the factory model? Do they continue to treat all students the same? Do they differentiate school experiences based on prior learning? To explore teachers' perspectives on educational equality, Wilbur Brookover and Lawrence Lezotte often asked teachers this question during an interview: "At the end of the day, it really doesn't matter who is president of the United States, governor of your state, or principal of your school; equal educational opportunity only has meaning when you close your classroom door and begin your work. What is your personal vision of what this important concept means for the students in your class?" Two very different visions would always emerge from the teachers' responses to this question. Many felt that equal educational opportunity in their class meant treating all the students the same. Others felt that equal educational opportunity meant treating each student in a manner fitting to his or her needs. A moment of reflection makes it clear that if one teacher holds one view and a second teacher the other, two very different visions of equal educational opportunity emerge. If these two teachers went into their classrooms and practiced their beliefs, the students' experiences and their learning outcomes would be very different.

The sameness standard that has traditionally dominated the structure and culture of public schools must be confronted if we are going to create and operate schools where all students have equal opportunities to learn. Customization and differentiation of instruction must be the focus of reform efforts designed to serve the learning needs of all students. Effective schools research and practices offer the best resources for embracing these two critical elements of education.

The Effective School Defined

We opened this chapter with our definition of an effective school and repeat it here to center attention on three concepts embedded in the definition: the learning-for-all mission, the focus on results, and the twin pillars of quality and equity.

The effective school is characterized by high overall student achievement with no significant gaps in that achievement across the major subgroups in the student population. The effective school is built on a foundation of high expectations, strong leadership, unwavering commitment to learning for all, collaboration, differentiated instruction, and frequent monitoring of student progress.

The Learning-for-All Mission

Shared acceptance and commitment to the learning-for-all mission by all stakeholders in a school is a prerequisite for ongoing success in both teaching and learning. This mission establishes a context in which the administration, the teaching faculty, the support staff, the students, and the larger community come together in their belief that everyone has a role in contributing to student achievement. The learning-for-all mission captures the passion that sustains effective schools. Schools that lack the passion for the learning-for-all mission may give lip service to the mission, and may even go through the motions of the effective schools process. Unfortunately, such schools will experience little, if any, success. Why? When staff members lack the belief in and commitment to learning for all, they will attribute student failure to external factors (for example, student ability, parental apathy, and student poverty) and feel less accountable for student success (McKenzie & Scheurich, 2008).

Focus on Results

Research has found repeatedly that leaders of effective schools understand that results are paramount. Educational leaders who are not ready to bet their legacy and maybe even their professional career on demonstrated student results, will be uncomfortable with the effective schools concept—and with good reason.

When educational leaders fully commit to the results paradigm, they embark upon a long and potentially explosive journey. Embracing the effective schools concept means that educators, policymakers, and other stakeholder groups must be prepared to address new questions: Which results should be collected? How should the desired results be gathered? When should the results be collected? Who makes the decisions, and how are the decisions communicated? In the final analysis, decisions are needed for each of these questions. Furthermore, the process for arriving at these decisions must be open so that all stakeholders are aware of the ramifications of the decisions for teaching and learning. Such openness is a hallmark of effective instructional leadership.

Quality and Equity

The twin policy pillars of public education—quality and equity—are integral to the concept of learning for all and must be considered simultaneously. Diane Ravitch, in her book *The Schools We Deserve* (1985), stated that link between quality and equality must be indissolvable. Each child in public school must be guaranteed a quality education *and* equal educational opportunity. Ravitch's passion for this idea is reflected in her assertion that whichever one of these two vital concepts a democracy chooses to ignore will bring down the democracy.

How do we create this strong link in a way that can serve to identify and describe the effective public school? Our definition of an effective school indicates that the proper connection is equity in quality: the effective school is characterized by high overall student achievement with no significant gaps in that achievement across the major subgroups in the student population. To determine if a school exhibits this necessary construct, an evaluator would first look at the school's indicators of quality (for example, number of advanced placement courses). Once the quality indicators have been identified, the evaluator would analyze those indicators to see who is participating in, and more importantly, benefiting from those centers of quality.

We offer a caveat regarding the definition of an effective school. The concept of the effective school as it has been employed in research and practice does not mean that "effectiveness" is an all-or-nothing concept. For example, a school, based on the outcome data examined, could be deemed effective in the curricular area of mathematics but not in the area of language arts. Such observations across subject areas can be very useful in verifying success and pointing to where more work is needed.

The Search for Effective Schools

The effective schools movement has used research to identify schools that exemplify the attributes of an effective school. Several methods of inquiry have been used to search for and identify effective schools, to study how such schools operate, and to determine the consequences for the students in these schools.

Looking at the methodological approaches is key to understanding the effective schools research and cultivating confidence in its findings.

The discourse in education is often complicated by varying interpretations of terms commonly used to report research findings or to engage in discussions about practice. To avoid miscommunication about effective schools research, we offer eight language lessons intended to establish a common vocabulary and shared meanings that will provide a foundation for the remainder of this book.

Language Lesson One—Effective, Efficient, Excellent

The terms *effective*, *efficient*, and *excellent* have been applied to schools and school-related research and are sometimes treated as synonyms. We use each of these terms in specific ways.

- *Effective* indicates that a school, teacher, or district is doing the right job. Based on our definition of an effective school, this term specifies that the school must attend to the twin policy pillars of quality and equity. Effective schools research has shown that the practices among effective schools have consistently been found to be more alike than different. Evidence of the similarities among effective schools has been found to be consistent across different levels of schools, rural, urban, and suburban schools, as well as in schools serving advantaged or disadvantaged students. It has often been said that effective schools are pretty much all alike, but an ineffective school is unique in its source of ineffectiveness.

- *Efficient* defines a school that is doing the right job in the right way. In the context of our discussion, an efficient school would be one in which staff drew upon the best research and proven practices to formulate and implement actions, processes, and programs. Although efficiency is an important characteristic, meeting the standard of effectiveness takes precedence over any meaningful consideration of efficiency. After all, what good is it to be efficient at the wrong thing?

- *Excellent* defines a school that is doing the right job, in the right way, and doing it better than most. The qualifier "excellent" implies the school is among the "best of the best." "Schools of excellence" is an expression commonly used in the field of effective schools research. In the search to identify and describe public schools of excellence, we would first need to locate a relatively large number of effective schools, and by the excellence criteria chosen, seek to identify and describe the best of the best among this cohort of schools as they demonstrate both quality and equity.

Language Lesson Two—School Effects Research, School Effectiveness Research, Effective Schools Research

When it comes to understanding a body of research that focuses on schools and schooling, three terms are often used, sometimes interchangeably, without making clear the differences between them: *school effects research*, *school effectiveness research*, and *effective schools research*. To understand the context for the effective schools research and practices, we think it is essential to appreciate the distinctions in the meanings of these terms. The relationships among the terms are illustrated in figure 1.1.

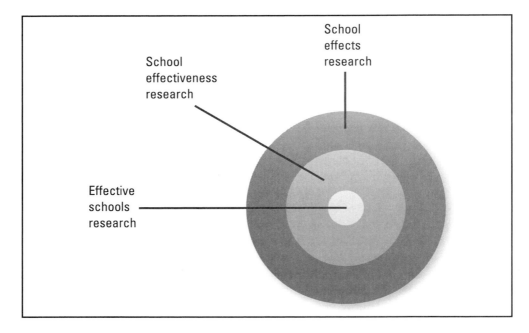

Figure 1.1: Critical research terms defined and differentiated.

- *School effects research* is used to describe any effect of schools or schooling that is found to be associated with attending school. It is the broadest of the three terms. Inquiries into school effects might look at the impact of noise levels in the classroom on the students' abilities to concentrate on their written work or to sustain time on assigned tasks. Such broad inquiries may be worthwhile and may ultimately contribute to the knowledge base for teaching and learning, but for the most part, they do not inform our understanding of particulars that define the effective school. School effects research represents the most inclusive body of school research and is represented by the outer circle in figure 1.1. This type of research is concerned with any school factors that are found to impact the students or staff in a school.

- *School effectiveness research* generally describes inquiries designed to study the relationship between some variable of interest (for example, class size) and some measured outcome (for example, student performance). Such inquiries are usually correlative and are designed to assess the strength of the relationship between one or more variables and one or more measured outcomes. A study of the relationship between class size in early elementary school and assessed performance on a national literacy test is an example of school effectiveness research. School effectiveness research is a subset of school effects research and is represented by the middle circle in figure 1.1. This research focuses specifically on the impact that selected variables have on student achievement.

School effects and school effectiveness methodologies are usually associated with such statistics as simple correlations, regression analysis, multiple regression analysis, and even more complex and sophisticated statistical techniques. These different types of inquires are undertaken using experimental or quasi-experimental research protocols. In the case of the experimental studies, students are randomly assigned to treatment groups (for example, classrooms with controlled noise levels) and control groups (classrooms where noise level is not controlled) and specified outcomes are measured (for example, student concentration). In quasi-experimental protocols, the students would not be randomly assigned to treatment groups; instead, existing classroom groups would be assigned to the various treatment conditions.

- *Effective schools research* analyzes the consequences of the inputs, processes, or curricular approaches on the various subsets of the pupil population served by the schools or classrooms contained in the study. Using methodologies similar to those used in school effectiveness research, the researcher in this case is interested in relating the effectiveness of a specific program, process, or strategy on an outcome of interest to determine ways in which those factors contribute to the school's success. Effective schools research contains two critical elements: (1) high overall levels of performance (quality) and (2) no gaps in the distribution of that performance across major subsets of the pupil population, for example, advantaged versus disadvantaged students (equity). Effective schools research is a subset of the school effectiveness work and is represented by the circle at the center of figure 1.1. This research is specifically concerned with the impact that selected variables have on various subgroups in the school (for example, boys' literacy achievement versus that of girls). Of the three forms of research described, this research is central to identifying schools that exemplify equity in quality of education.

Language Lesson Three—Data Disaggregation

The effective school and associated research represent a framework for judging a school and its programs or services. Effective schools researchers have been credited (or condemned) with inventing the term *data disaggregation*. Data disaggregation involves dividing a body of data into segments. For example, test scores for an entire student population are examined according to various factors characteristic of subgroups in that population, including economic status, gender, race, ethnicity, disability, and primary language. This concept of disaggregation rose out of the notion that without looking specifically at the impact of the school's offerings on the various subgroups served, one cannot accurately and appropriately judge whether the school is performing effectively. As Ron Edmonds so aptly put it, "Schools cannot be judged effective if a significant portion of the pupil population fails to demonstrate mastery" (1982, p. 9).

Disaggregating student achievement data has become one of the most iden-tifiable cornerstones of the effective schools concept and research. Prior to the effective schools studies of the 1980s, educators tended to look at assessed student achievement in the aggregate. If they disaggregated the data at all, they tended to look at the student data for boys and girls. Few schools or districts had the desire or courage to look at the student performance data through the lenses of race, ethnic-ity, or socioeconomic status. For decades, most educators failed to understand how disaggregation would add value to their school improvement efforts. Because of the increasing emphasis of federal and state government on more stringent standards and greater accountability, most educational leaders now recognize that disaggre-gation is a powerful *problem-finding* strategy. Notice we didn't say *problem-solving* strategy. Identifying the problem is key to the learning-for-all mission, since virtu-ally every problem-solving strategy must begin with an accurate description of the problem. Disaggregation of student performance data provides that description.

Language Lesson Four—Outliers

In the earliest studies of effective schools, researchers used a specific method-ology known today as the study of outliers. In his book *Outliers*, author Malcolm Gladwell provided two definitions for this term, both of which are appropriate in understanding the effective schools research:

> Definition #1—"Something (or someone) that is situated away from or classified differently from a main or related body."
>
> Definition #2—"A statistical observation that is markedly different in value from the others of the sample." (2008, p. 2)

The search for and description of outliers as a research methodology can and has been used in a variety of settings other than the study of effective schools. Tom Peters and Robert Waterman, in their book *In Search of Excellence* (1982), described businesses that were unusually successful in their market niche. Once they identified such businesses, Peters and Waterman set out to determine what policies, practices, and procedures seemed to explain their "positive deviant" or outlier status. In an effort to describe how the outlier businesses were different, the researchers studied comparable businesses that were not as successful. This research proved to be popular in the business sector for several years, and it influ-enced thinking about the role of outliers in school effectiveness research. More recently, Jim Collins and his research team conducted a study of contemporary outlier businesses and described their findings in *Good to Great* (2002). Like Peters and Waterman, Collins followed the outlier methodology, but used a different defi-nition of greatness. Collins focused on businesses that were not always unusually successful, but became so over time and remained so for an extended period of time. The Collins work has dominated the narrative in the business world for a few years now, and has garnered interest with educators, especially those concerned with instructional coaching (Knight, 2007).

Gladwell (2008), in contrast to others who have used the outlier methodology, examined a variety of different types of outliers. He compared and contrasted individuals who have been unusually effective in a particular career field. He also described communities where rates of illness are unusually low compared to other communities.

The effective schools researchers used outlier methodology to investigate schools that served large proportions of poor or minority students that distinguished themselves from the norm because of their markedly higher achievement. We have summarized many of these studies in Effective Schools Research LiNK, a twenty-year online research archive where you can find abstracts of outlier studies of unusually effective teachers, superintendents, schools, and districts.

The use of the outlier methodology in a variety of fields and settings is a testament to its legitimacy and validity as an approach to disciplined inquiry. However, some critics of the outlier methodology claim that it is nontheoretical, that it doesn't show us how the effective organizations came to be so, and thus doesn't enable other organizations to replicate their successes. While the criticism has some validity, the fact is that insights garnered from outlier research have been overwhelmingly beneficial in creating effective reform strategies.

To be credible, inquiry in any field that uses the outlier methodology must start with a clear definition of the criteria that will be used to judge unusual effectiveness. While we acknowledge the value of outlier methodology, we caution readers to pay very close attention to the operational definition or criterion used to assess outlier status in effective school studies.

Effective School Milestones: The Challenge

As noted in the introduction, the effective schools research was launched in July 1966 in response to a finding reported in the Equal Educational Opportunity Study (Coleman, 1966). The study, commissioned by the United States Congress, looked at the allocation of resources and the effectiveness of instruction in American schools in relation to racial composition. The study's findings prompted wide discussion and a variety of interpretations. One of the most controversial features of the study related to the implication that schools made little difference in the education of minority and poor children in America. Instead, family background appeared to be the major determinant of student achievement. By lending credence to the idea that schools made little difference in student achievement, the report stimulated a vigorous reaction, instigating many of the studies that would later come to define the research base for the effective schools movement. The educational researchers who conducted these studies developed a body of research that supported the premise that all children can learn and that the school controls the factors necessary to ensure student mastery of the core curriculum.

Investigating the question of whether or not schools make a difference in the achievement of children has turned out to be a thriving movement that continues today, more than forty years after it started. The quest to determine what makes a school effective has evolved through several significant stages. Understanding these changes helps to understand where the movement is today and where it is likely to go in future. The phases overlap somewhat, as the transition between them occurred over time.

Phase I: Identification (1960s to Mid-1970s)

The best (and perhaps only) evidence that could actually challenge the EEO Study findings that schools serving poor and minority students didn't make a difference was to identify schools that did seem to make a difference for poor and minority children. It seemed that the best way to conduct such studies was to find two schools with similar-sized student bodies, similar proportions of minority and poor students, and comparable resource inputs, with one school demonstrating significantly higher measured achievement than the other. The key question was: could such high-achieving schools be found? Several researchers, Ron Edmonds, Wilbur Brookover, and Lawrence Lezotte among them, initially operating independently of one another, began to go in search of schools that seemed to defy the Coleman conclusion.

Michigan was one of the first states to develop and administer statewide, curricular-based, criterion-referenced assessments of all students in selected grades in all public schools. As a result, Michigan was one of the first states where the search for effective schools was even feasible. Because of the expansion of state assessment programs, effective schools research studies now can (and should) be conducted in every state. While the Michigan assessment results were routinely made available to the schools after being scored, segmenting those results was a demanding task at a time when computer technology was limited. Nevertheless, it was possible to examine the achievement profiles of the schools on the state assessments relative to the demographic profile of the students who attended each school. For example, researchers could estimate the number of poor children attending the school by examining the number of students receiving a free or reduced-price lunch. The goal was to find those schools with high concentrations of disadvantaged students (minority or nonminority) and find a comparable school where the input profiles were similar but the achievement profiles were not as positive. Examples of these especially effective schools were found repeatedly, in varying locations, and in both large and small communities.

Phase 2: The Descriptive Phase (1970s to Mid-1980s)

The search for and identification of the effective schools in the early studies captured the interest of the research community. While educational practitioners were only mildly interested in this sort of academic research, it did prompt them to ask, "How did these schools do it?" "How are these schools different from most other schools serving poor and minority students?" These questions prompted the researchers to enter the second major phase of the movement, the descriptive phase. The focus during this time was on studying the inner workings of these effective schools to determine why these schools were clearly outliers when it came to the education of poor and minority children.

To investigate what happened in schools, a field research team went into the schools to conduct interviews, surveys, and direct observations (Brookover & Lezotte, 1977). When the field research team returned from the schools, they recorded everything they learned about the effective schools on one wall and the data from the comparison schools on the other. The analysis took the form of asking the question, "What attributes do the effective schools have in common with each other that are not shared by the comparison schools?"

Ron Edmonds (1979) published a study designed to identify and analyze schools that provided effective instruction for poor and minority children, and to establish the relationship between student family background and school effectiveness. This study, which included a reanalysis of the 1966 Equal Educational Opportunity Study data (Fredericksen, 1975), indicated that differences in performance between effective and ineffective schools could not be attributed to differences in the social class and family background of pupils enrolled in those schools. This finding was in sharp contrast to that of the EEO Study, which minimized the role of schooling. Edmonds's findings were quickly validated in other studies of the effective outlier schools. Based on his own work and that of other effective schools researchers, Edmonds identified and described what he called the "characteristics of effective schools" (1979, p. 15). Researchers found that every effective school had strong instructional leadership, conveyed a strong sense of mission, demonstrated effective instructional behaviors, held high expectations for all students, practiced frequent monitoring of student achievement, and operated in a safe and orderly manner. These shared attributes eventually became known as the correlates of effective schools. Edmonds noted that "to advance school effectiveness, a school must implement all of the characteristics at once" (1982, p. 9).

The effective schools research studies in both the identification and descriptive phases of the movement in the United States focused primarily on elementary schools. In England, the initial effective schools study that received wide acclaim focused on secondary schools. These findings were reported in a book titled *Fifteen Thousand Hours: Secondary Schools and Their Effects on Children* (Rutter, Maughan, Mortimore, & Outston, 1979). In the ensuing years, researchers in many countries have contributed to the mosaic of effective school studies.

Phase 3: The Prescriptive Phase (1985–1995)

When the studies describing the effective schools correlates began to appear in the professional education literature, the world of the effective schools researchers changed dramatically. Their telephones began to ring off the hook with calls from local school principals and superintendents. The question no longer focused on how the effective schools were different. Now the question was, "Can you come to our school or district and guide us in making our schools effective?"

The Michigan State University team of effective schools researchers was honored by these requests, but a bit unsure as to how to respond. Remember, when the researchers found effective schools "in nature," as it were, these schools were already effective. Furthermore, when the researchers discovered the correlates of effective schools present and strong in the effective schools, these attributes were already there when they arrived. The original research provided little guidance as to how the effective schools became effective; that is, how the processes evolved or how the correlates came into place. Discovering the outlier as it existed in schools identified as effective is one thing; it's quite another to tell someone how to *create* an effective school. The researchers had confidence in their descriptions, but those descriptions didn't define the steps they should prescribe to interested school leaders. In the more common language of the 1980s, the effective schools research provided a vision of a more desirable place for schools to be but gave little insight as to how best to make the journey to that place.

To resolve this dilemma, researchers started with the assumption that if they were going to ask school leaders to use their research as a way of improving their school or district, they should use research to guide themselves in developing a recommended process. This situation presented a new question for effective schools researchers: what research should be used to help frame a research-based process for guiding the schools and districts seeking help? Previous effective schools research provided insights into ways to conceptualize school improvement efforts. Each conceptualization suggested a different body of research to consider, which researchers subsequently found to be interrelated and mutually reinforcing (Edmonds, 1982; Good & Brophy, 1991; Levine & Lezotte, 1990).

First, it was clear that if schools were going to become effective, the behaviors of the staff would need to change to some degree. In this case, school improvement equals people change. That conclusion led to an examination of the research on effective staff development models and effective training models. Second, if schools were going to become effective, the organization or system would have to change to some degree as well. That conclusion led to an examination of the best available research on organizational development. Finally, the researchers concluded that whether it's people change or organizational change, the change must be planned. This realization led to an examination of the best available models of planned change.

We can draw several conclusions about the nature of change from these three different concepts and their supporting research:

- Change takes time and must be viewed as a process, not an event.
- Sustainable change requires commitment by the people that have to do the changing.
- Involving those who are affected by the change in the actual change process is one of the best ways to build ownership, buy-in, and sustained commitment.

- Leadership is critical in providing both the vision and the support for the changes that are needed to make it happen.

- Effective leadership is a necessary (but not sufficient) condition.

The integration of the effective schools research findings with the guiding process principles led to organizing a data-driven and results-oriented change process around a collaborative leadership team. To increase the level of involvement and, at the same time, bring the research into the school, the process also included formation of correlate teams (one team for each correlate).

The number of schools and districts that purported to initiate programs of school improvement based on the effective schools research is in the hundreds, if not thousands. The researchers at Michigan State University only worked with a relatively small percentage of the total, since others also took up the challenge. What we don't know is how many of the schools that claimed they were implementing the effective schools process did so with real fidelity and quality. Many schools and districts implemented the concepts in name only, with limited results. On the other hand, we know of many cases where the process was implemented with care, and the results were impressive.

Phase 4: The School District (1985–1995)

The effective schools research originally focused on the single school and not the school district. When someone would ask, "What is the role of the central office, superintendent, or board of education in creating effective schools?" the initial response was that the roles were irrelevant! This response was based on the fact that when researchers found an effective school, it was likely in a district with many other schools, none of which were effective, yet all had the same board, superintendent, and central office. This situation seemed to negate the influence of the central office on the individual school. Also, it seemed clear that a school staff could implement the correlates of effective schools at any time, with no particular outside help or support. In the schools that were already found to be effective, researchers found no evidence of outside help or support. While this position in many ways was correct, effective schools researchers subsequently tempered their view.

It is true that schools come to be effective one school at a time. However, it is also true that it is very difficult to sustain the effective school without the support of the central office, superintendent, and board of education. Years of working with schools convinced researchers that district support was indispensable for a school to be able to maintain its effective status. They found that, without broad-based organizational support, school effectiveness depended too heavily on the heroic commitment of the school leader (the principal) or only a few dedicated staff. Researchers witnessed numerous cases in which the principal of an effective school moved on and was replaced by someone who did not share the passion, vision, or values of the previous administrator. When that happened, the school usually returned to its earlier state quickly.

As a result of these observations, researchers made a midcourse correction in their approach to assisting schools with programs of school improvement based on the effective schools research. With support from the U.S. Office of Education, the Michigan State University team, in collaboration with local school improvement experts, developed a two-pronged approach to school improvement. One track was designed to train and empower school-level collaborative teams to plan and implement school improvement based on the research. The second track focused on a district-level leadership team that included the superintendent. This team was charged with the responsibility of developing and subsequently implementing a district plan designed to support the school-by-school process. Clearly, this dual effort was intended to increase the likelihood that schools that became effective would remain so even if the school leader changed.

Hundreds of school district teams have been trained on the effective schools process. The results represented good news and bad news. The good news was that many more schools were able to realize significant progress because they received assurances and support from the central office and the superintendent. The bad news was that if the superintendent left, the replacement would often be a person who did not have the passion, share the vision, or offer the support needed to sustain the district effort. Consequently, school districts that had taken two steps forward would quickly take two steps back. To this day, it is a struggle to build continuity and stability in some districts because, in spite of the standards and accountability movement, district leaders are usually given the authority to put their own brand on the organization, regardless of whether or not the earlier brand was working.

Phase 5: Total System Alignment (1995–Present)

As we follow the history of the effective schools movement from the earliest days to the present, it is easy to see how it has become more inclusive and expansive. For example, virtually every state has developed some results-oriented accountability system. Many of the states have required or at least encouraged schools to plan and implement programs of school reform based on the effective schools research and proven practices. In addition, most of the regional accreditation models require schools to document the processes and practices based, in whole or in part, on effective schools research. Many of the provisions that the effective schools proponents have been advocating since the earliest days of the movement were incorporated as key tenets of the 2001 No Child Left Behind legislation. In fact, despite the controversy surrounding NCLB, it was the first time the learning-for-all mission was recognized at a national level. With this being so, it seems reasonable to claim that most of the crucial elements of the system at large are now aligned and leaders at both the school and district levels are focused on the same outcomes.

However, higher education is one part of the system that is still on the fence when it comes to alignment with the rest of the system. When it comes to public education, higher education has a great deal of power and influence. It controls who gets admitted to colleges, and it trains and certifies teachers and administrators. Unfortunately, if we are to believe our colleagues in schools, most of these institutions are not yet doing what needs to be done to prepare students or staff for the challenges of 21st century education.

The journey from 1966 to the present represents a history of successes in helping more schools be more effective in helping more students be successful. For that we can and should be proud. On the other hand, the journey from 1966 to the present is a story of starts and stops when it comes to sustainable change in our public schools. The resistance evidenced by the system in place all along the journey is testimony to the stability of the current system. Stability is good when the system is doing what is best for all students and, in turn, society. Stability becomes the enemy when it negates and impedes opportunities to implement proven practices for school improvement.

Conclusion

We've all heard the expression, "If you don't know where you're going, any road will get you there." Perhaps a fitting corollary might be: "If you don't know where you're going or where you've been, you're truly lost." In this chapter, we've provided both a historical and social-political context for the effective schools concept and research. Examining (even briefly) the path that public schools have traveled to get from where they started to where they are today represents an important contextual framework for deeper study of the effective schools concepts, research, and practices.

Effective schools research has contributed to the school reform movement and influenced changes in public education. These developments are taken for granted today, but that was not always the case. The developments include:

- Using disaggregated data to simultaneously attend to quality and equity

- Using achievement results, rather than processes or programs, to judge the effectiveness of the schools

- Developing more data-driven systems with leaders who have had to become knowledgeable about this approach

- Recognizing that collaboration and ownership among the staff are necessary to successfully initiate and sustain school improvement

- Realizing and accepting that change is a complex process that takes time, effort, and commitment

- Understanding that, when it comes to sustainable change in schools and districts, all the stakeholders have to be a part of the dialogue and the changes that follow

Since the 1970s, hundreds of schools and districts have used the effective schools research as the foundation for school improvement efforts. This research continues to be used by more and more schools in response to federal and state accountability programs. This body of work remains central to the discourse of school reform for two main reasons. First, the vision of the effective school is the correct vision for our time—high overall levels of achievement and no gaps in the distribution of that achievement across all the student subgroups. Second, as the body of work has evolved, the research has described in great detail the critical variables that are consistently found to be associated with school effectiveness. These variables have come to be known as the correlates of effective schools. These characteristics have been so pervasive among effective schools that we have come to recognize that the extent to which they are present within a school is a strong indicator as to its effectiveness.

CHAPTER 2

A Systems Approach to the Correlates of Effective Schools

The effective school is a complex system of manageable, interdependent components propelled by broad staff commitment to successfully accomplish the mission of learning for all.

The School as a System

During the Prescriptive Phase (1985–1995) of the effective schools movement, researchers began to consider relevant research contributions from other fields, including systems organization. The noted author and father of the Total Quality Movement, W. Edwards Deming defined "a system as a *network of interdependent components that work together to accomplish the aim of the system*" (1993, p. 51, italics added). Clearly, the individual school more than qualifies as a system. From the moment students arrive at school until they return home at the end of the school day, they encounter several components that constitute the school as a system. These components include transportation, the classroom, the lunchroom, and perhaps medical, guidance, or disciplinary services. Presumably, each and every one of these separate components is working together to accomplish the aim of the system.

According to Deming, to be viable, a system must meet three standards: (1) the system must have a clear aim, purpose, or mission; (2) it must be able to be managed; and finally, (3) a broad-based commitment to the aim must be evident throughout the system. Each of these standards can be applied to the school as a system.

The Aim of the System

Public schools, individually and in the collective sense, have always struggled to be clear about what constitutes the primary aim or mission. This problem is particularly evident in American public schools, which, unlike schools in some other countries, are used for many social purposes. For example, American schools must provide transportation, feed children, provide sports and extracurricular activities, and prepare students for the future, as well as serve as a place for desegregating students who live in neighborhoods that are largely segregated.

Effective schools researchers have generally characterized the competing missions facing public schools in three broad categories: (1) custodial care, (2) teaching and learning, and (3) sorting and selecting. While there is room for all three of these purposes on the mission's "bus," only one of them can *drive* the bus. The Effective Schools philosophy takes the view that the primary aim of the public school is that of teaching and learning, and the others must be seen as being in service to it. In fact, each interdependent component within the educational system must be judged in terms of its ability to add value to the primary learning mission of teaching and learning.

Managing the Aim

Most schools have developed measuring and data-gathering systems about the performance of the custodial and sorting missions. The custodial mission can be managed through such data as attendance records, disciplinary reports, and immunization reports. The sorting mission can be managed by monitoring data on the number of graduates who go to college, the number of students who drop out, or the number of students in the gifted and talented program. The findings from effective schools research have been instrumental in helping educators look more closely at performance measures and data gathering tools to monitor the learning mission.

Measuring student performance as a way of managing the learning mission is quite new in the history of education. Until the standards and accountability movement began to build on effective schools research, few (if any) of the metrics and data-gathering and reporting systems were used to monitor the learning mission. Today, the majority of states and provinces in North America have developed assessment systems that provide at least an annual measure of student proficiency. Although use of high-stakes assessments has been controversial at times, there does not appear to be any broad-based desire to eliminate those tests. In spite of the criticisms and problems with standardized assessments, they have prompted schools to engage in ongoing monitoring of student achievement. This is only the first step, though. To become truly effective, schools must move beyond the level of annual assessments to ongoing assessment of each child's progress. That will require a monitoring system as sophisticated, thorough, and matter-of-fact about analyzing measures of student performance as they currently are about measuring and monitoring attendance.

Technological advances in data-gathering and reporting have made it possible for educators to create systems that ensure that both teaching and learning occur in school. By disaggregating student performance data, educators can determine who is benefiting from the programs, programs that reflect the school's learning mission. The future looks bright regarding the ability of schools to manage the learning mission. We have the tools, all we need is the sustained commitment to do so, which brings us to Deming's third component of a system.

Broad-Based Commitment to the Mission

If we believe what educators say when they are asked to state the mission of their school, we might conclude that their commitment to the learning-for-all mission is more evident today than in the past. This is a good sign. On the other hand, many educators hold negative views about tests currently used to monitor and measure the learning mission. These views seem to contradict the expressed commitment to the learning mission. Noting that high-stakes assessments have been in place for more than a decade, we are prompted to ask what leads educators to be so critical of efforts to define the success (or failure) of the learning mission. If the issue was about the measures and not the mission itself, wouldn't we expect that, by now, educational groups would have developed more acceptable forms of measuring the mission? These questions and attendant speculations cannot be ignored, since a viable system must have broad-based support among those who must deliver the mission.

Systemic Forces For and Against Change

Underperforming or less-effective schools are under siege today. These schools have not been successful in dealing with changes in society, nor have their leaders taken advantage of the available research that defines success. Consequently, such schools do not keep pace with others where society's expectations are being realized. The current system faces several competing challenges. Figure 2.1 (page 32) illustrates systemic forces that both drive and resist efforts at school change. The driving forces are relatively new, but they are powerful because they are grounded in society's longstanding belief in equality of opportunity for all students. The forces of resistance are grounded in keeping things the way things have always been, as well as a fundamental doubt that all children can learn. The system has a great deal of inertia to do again what it has always done, and the forces for change will need to be stronger and more persistent to significantly alter the system.

The Role of the Correlates in the System

The correlates are critical to the effective school because they represent the leading organizational and contextual indicators that have been shown to influence student learning. The extent to which the correlates are in place in a school has a dramatic, positive effect on student achievement. Over the years, the effective schools researchers have been both surprised and impressed with how durable these correlates have proven to be across time and settings.

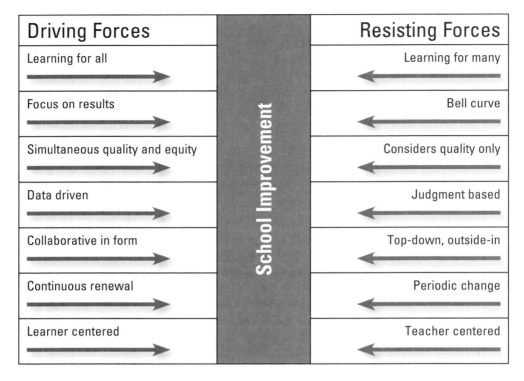

Driving Forces	School Improvement	Resisting Forces
Learning for all		Learning for many
Focus on results		Bell curve
Simultaneous quality and equity		Considers quality only
Data driven		Judgment based
Collaborative in form		Top-down, outside-in
Continuous renewal		Periodic change
Learner centered		Teacher centered

Figure 2.1: Forces affecting school improvement efforts.

To truly appreciate the usefulness of the effective schools correlates in framing a comprehensive and continuous school improvement strategy, two additional contextual concepts need to be briefly discussed: (1) learner-centered systems and (2) leading indicators. These two concepts provide the compelling infrastructure that makes it easier for school leaders to cross from research to school reform practices.

Teacher-Centered Versus Learner-Centered Systems

Robert Branson identified what he called the "theory of upper limits" (1987). According to Branson's theory, in any system there is an upper limit of capacity as to what that system can produce. As a system approaches its upper limit, it requires more and more inputs to produce smaller and smaller increases in productivity or outputs. Branson concluded that schools, as we know them, have been and are currently what he calls a teacher-centered system. In this system, the majority of the resources are organized around the teacher and teaching. He also observed that the current teacher-centered system is performing at about 95 percent of its capacity and is approaching its upper limit. He suggests that to realize the last 5 percent of the potential in the current teacher-centered system's capacity would require nearly doubling the input resources—an unlikely future indeed.

Branson's theory states that whenever a system approaches its upper limit, leaders tend to search for a new system or paradigm. Given the new mission of learning for all and the problem of approaching the upper limits in the current system, Branson suggests that the new paradigm for schools ought to be a learner-centered system. Branson (2000, p. 5) asserts, "Teacher-centered, classroom-controlled instruction is represented in both past and present models. Learner-centered, performance-paced instruction, adapted to each student, is represented in the future model. This paradigm shift *must occur* before substantial improvements can be made and retained" [italics added].

To design and implement a viable learner-centered system, leaders must build the new paradigm based on the knowledge associated with human learning. As soon as school leaders become good students of the human learning research, they quickly realize that the current teacher-centered system stands in obvious contradiction to many of the principles coming from the research on human learning. With this realization in hand, these leaders must confront the obvious fork in the road: are educational leaders going to press on and continue to try to make the current teacher-centered system work better, or are they going to begin the process of transforming the system into a learner-centered system? If the answer is transforming the system to learner-centered, then school leaders will have to address some of the apparent contradictions between the two different perspectives. These contradictions include placing students in learning groups based on age rather than prior knowledge, assuming that the time for teaching is constant even though some students need more time than others, and ignoring the power of individualized feedback as a powerful learning strategy.

The correlates of effective schools represent organizational or systemic strategies for aligning the student's learning experiences with many of the principles of human learning on a schoolwide basis. When the correlates are implemented across the school, their ability to add value to student learning is beyond what a single teacher can do working alone.

From a conversation with Madeline Hunter, Larry Lezotte recalls her comments about effective teaching and effective schools. Hunter, a pioneer in effective teaching research, clearly described the relationship between the effective schools correlates and effective teaching principles. She asserted that effective schools research, when put into practice, represents the organizational umbrella under which effective teaching can flourish. Make no mistake; there is nothing more important than the teacher-student relationship. On the other hand, in an effective organizational culture, school leaders will find it much easier to make effective teaching practices an ongoing, everyday phenomenon in the school.

Leading Versus Trailing Indicators of a System

The standards and accountability movement of the last decade has caused school leaders to focus on student performance explicitly when planning and implementing school improvement programs. Unfortunately, most of the school leaders quickly realize that focusing on past results, as important as they are, does not provide much guidance as to what the leaders should change in order to

improve future measured student performance. This is in keeping with the observations of Deming (1993), who noted that a system's performance cannot be
improved very much by focusing on its results alone.

The performance results reflected in assessment scores are what an economist
would call a *trailing indicator*. To improve a system's performance, educators must
focus on the *leading indicators*. Leading indicators are those factors that cause or
significantly influence the trailing indicators of productivity or performance. In
the context of education, measured student achievement is clearly an after-the-
fact or trailing indicator of student learning. To improve student performance,
educators must leverage changes in the leading indicators of student learning. If
the school is successful in modifying the leading indicators, student performance
will improve.

What are the important leading indicators of school learning that need to be
changed to improve student learning and performance? There are two primary
sources that educators should consider: (1) the principles of human learning and
(2) the correlates of effective schools. These two sets of leading indicators are
mutually reinforcing and combine to provide powerful strategies for improving
student performance in our schools. Our focus centers on the correlates of effective schools; however, readers who want to pursue information about student
learning may want to refer to *How Students Learn: History, Mathematics, and Science
in the Classroom* (Donovan & Bransford, 2005).

Interdependence Among the Correlates

Two questions usually arise when considering the interdependence of the correlates and how that factor plays into decisions about implementing them:

1. Can the correlates be implemented one at a time and in serial fashion?
2. Which correlate is the most important?

Because the correlates are interdependent, school leaders must approach them
with the intention of implementing them all at once. Some schools have tried
to ignore the interdependence factor, only to be frustrated because the resulting
progress is so slow. It would probably be easier for educators to work with the
correlates one after the other, but that approach does not work very well. For
example, how could we strengthen the correlate of high expectations for success
and at the same time leave the correlate of opportunity to learn/time on task for
another day? High expectations only qualify as high expectations when they cause
some change in the opportunity and time allocation structures in the classroom
and school.

Which correlate is or will prove to be the most important when it comes to
improving schools and student learning? This question has spurred many spir-
ited debates. The correlate of strong instructional leadership has tended to gather

a large constituency. Others have advocated for the correlate of positive home-school relations.

Even Ron Edmonds and Larry Lezotte, who frequently talked about these matters, had different answers to the question of which correlate would ultimately emerge as the most important. While the two researchers always focused on the interdependent nature of the correlates and attempted to duck and dodge the question, they weren't always successful. In the spirit of candor, Lezotte always speculated that future research would find that the correlate of high expectations for success would prove to be the most important. His logic was that one had to start with high expectations for success grounded in the belief that all students can learn; otherwise, he couldn't imagine how any other correlate would energize the effective school system into place.

Larry recalls that Ron Edmonds would often follow with his view, saying, "If a school's motives are right, the most important correlate would turn out to be the frequent monitoring of progress." His logic went as follows: if the school has the proper motives and pays attention to the results it is achieving, eventually all the other correlates will be driven into place. When pressed to address what he meant when he said, "If a school's motives are right," Edmonds would answer, "If a school has high expectations grounded in the belief that all children can learn!" Over time, it seems that each correlate has acquired its own supporters who provide logical reasons for its importance in school improvement efforts. A case can be made for each one. On the other hand, the interdependent nature of the subsystems means that, at the end of the day, one has to be prepared to see the correlates as a set and not standalone components.

Public and Private Systems

The systems perspective has been used to describe how private, for-profit companies—large or small—need to view their work processes. People who work in such settings are usually very comfortable with the ideas associated with systems thinking. Unfortunately, the systems perspective is not as widely understood or used when it comes to thinking about educational institutions generally, and public schools specifically. Educators who reject the systems idea often do so because of their concerns that findings from research conducted in the context of businesses do not effectively translate into what is needed in schools. As a result, most schools approach school reform in a piecemeal fashion—without regard to the entire system—and realize only partial success. Systems thinking offers key benefits to schools seeking to become more effective, allowing them to take a comprehensive approach to improvement and address underlying causes of inadequate student achievement.

Educational leaders would be well advised and well served to become students of systems thinking. Those school leaders who attempt to lead without understanding the school as a system, and the systemic problems that are currently associated with it, are bound to be frustrated and experience only modest improvement.

Conclusion

The correlates of effective schools represent a set of interdependent components that work together to accomplish the aim of the effective school: learning for all. In this respect, the correlates contribute to the functioning of a school as a system. The standards that characterize an effective system apply to schools: clearly defined mission, the means to monitor and manage the mission, and broad-based commitment to the mission. Each correlate can be viewed as a necessary subsystem that meets these standards and that contributes to the overall effectiveness of the school. In part II (chapters 3 through 9) of this book, we describe the correlates one at a time. While it is useful to consider the correlates individually for purposes of becoming familiar with the related research, remember that each is a necessary, but not sufficient part of a system that successfully produces learning for all.

PART II

The Correlates of Effective Schools Defined

CHAPTER 3

High Expectations for Success

In the effective school, staff members believe that all students can and will obtain mastery of the intended curriculum and in their professional capacity to enable all students to achieve mastery.

It has been said that, in life, you may not get all that you want but, more often than not, you get what you expect. The power of expectations is equally true in schools when it comes to student learning and success. Students' beliefs about their own abilities to succeed influence what they expect will occur during their learning experiences in school. Likewise, teachers' and administrators' beliefs, relative to the educability of their students, influence what they expect will occur during the students' encounters with teaching and profoundly impact their behavior toward students. In turn, adult expectations have a profound influence on how the students come to see themselves as learners and their likely success in school.

The effects of teacher expectations are captured in this observation from *The MetLife Survey of the American Teacher* (2009):

> Educators have long been aware of the 'Pygmalion effect' in schools—the process through which students whose teachers expect them to learn do, and those not expected to learn do not. Teacher pessimism about students in poorly functioning schools is likely to result in the 'Pygmalion effect' working negatively in schools which are currently serving their students poorly.

High expectations for success is an individual and institutional mindset. In her best-selling book *Mindset: The New Psychology of Success* (2006), Carol Dweck provides a detailed description of the two dominate mindsets that continue to have a profound effect on educators' views of the classroom and the educability of the students. Some educators operate from the view that student learning and student achievement are the result of fixed intelligence, which is innate, unalterable, and predetermined. Other educators approach their work with a growth mindset—the view that intelligence develops over time through experiences and, therefore, is subject to influence. Whichever mindset educators bring to the teaching-and-learning setting strongly impacts their actions in the classroom and their expectations for students.

Because mindsets are internal and private, they are elusive and impossible to observe directly. Nonetheless, the impact of expectations conveyed by different mindsets cannot be overstated. A poor child who happens to find himself with a teacher who believes in the fixed intelligence mindset will have very different classroom experiences from those he will have with a growth-mindset teacher.

In the early days of the effective schools movement, the correlate was identified simply as "high expectations." "For success" was added to clarify the difference between high *standards* and high *expectations*. The need for clarification was prompted by the confusion created by the higher standards movement that began in the 1990s.

For the effective schools researchers, standards represent those external hurdles that we expect students to meet. On the other hand, high expectations represent those beliefs about whether all students can successfully meet the standards set for them. If confronted with an either/or choice between standards and expectations (which we are not advocating), an educator would do well to choose high expectations, since they are far more life changing than high standards. The history of humankind is replete with stories of "mountains" being moved by high expectations. On the other hand, lives are rarely changed by high standards alone.

The definition of high expectations for success has two critical elements. The first element focuses on the staff's beliefs about students' ability to succeed: the staff believes that all students can and will obtain mastery of the intended curriculum. The second element addresses the staff's sense of efficacy. Sense of efficacy is the belief that one can successfully achieve what one is being asked to do. In the effective school, the staff members believe in their individual and collective professional capacity to enable all students to achieve mastery. A teacher's sense of efficacy is positively related to student success in learning and achievement (Scribner, 1999; Weber & Omotani, 1994). This implies that high expectations for student success begin with teachers first having high expectations for themselves—confidence that they possess the necessary knowledge and skills to provide students with quality learning experiences.

Changing the level of expectations that defines a school's climate is one of the most challenging correlates to implement. Why is this so? High expectations have been described as *unwarranted optimism*. In this context, it means that the teachers individually and the staff collectively generally believe that the students can and will succeed, even in the face of evidence to the contrary. A teacher can plan a lesson, teach the lesson to the best of her ability, see that some students succeed and others do not, and conclude that those who didn't succeed are not capable of learning (McKenzie & Scheurich, 2008). Holding on to the belief that all can learn and all will learn in the face of such evidence illustrates what is meant by *unwarranted optimism*. Holding on to high expectations in the face of countervailing evidence is difficult for even one person to do, but it becomes even more challenging for an entire school staff. Nevertheless, persisting in the belief that all can and will succeed—what Hoy, Tarter, and Hoy (2006) call *academic optimism*—is critical to fulfilling the learning-for-all mission.

Schoolwide Efficacy and Expectations

Teachers can and do have different expectations for individual students or groups of students. We also know that teachers develop their sense of professional efficacy individually. They have their own views as to whether they believe that they can successfully do what is being asked of them as teachers (Guskey & Passaro, 1994). In addition, we know that some teachers in a school may have a sense of efficacy different from their colleagues in the school (Goddard, Hoy, & Hoy, 2000). A new and exciting line of inquiry has begun around the question, "Do schools develop a schoolwide sense of efficacy?" (Goddard, Hoy, & Hoy, 2004). This question stems from the primary focus of the standards and accountability movement on the single school.

When researchers began this line of inquiry, they tried estimating teacher efficacy for a school by adding up the individual teacher scores on surveys and calculating the average. The results of this strategy were disappointing and confusing; disappointing because the average efficacy scores revealed little variability from school to school, and confusing because these scores seemed to have no correlation with achievement and achievement gains in the schools.

As a result, researchers changed their strategy and a whole different picture emerged. In the first studies, the researchers asked teachers: "Do you believe that you can successfully do what is being asked of you?" In the second round of studies, the question was rephrased: "Do you believe that you and your colleagues as a whole can successfully do what is being asked of this school?" The wording change yielded a different picture. The researchers found that this efficacy measurement correlated far more strongly with levels of achievement and achievement gains, and varied greatly among schools (Goddard, Logerfo, & Hoy, 2004). Schools that had higher levels of *collective* efficacy showed higher levels of achievement.

Why would the outcome of this inquiry be so different? In the first case, the respondents could honestly indicate that they believed that they, as individual teachers, could do what was being asked of them. However, the unspoken prerequisite is "if only my colleagues would successfully do what is being expected of *them*." In the second case, the respondents had to see their efficacy not as individuals, but as members of a larger accountable community. The results are a gauge of the confidence of the individual teachers in both their colleagues and the system as a whole to accomplish the learning-for-all mission.

The Roots of Educational Expectations

The mindset about student ability that educators bring to their professional activities can have a significant impact on the expectations they have for students, the ways in which they teach, and their interactions with students. Some people believe that innate ability is the primary determinant of school learning and school achievement—that ability is inherited, fixed at birth, and unalterable. Others tend to see ability as the outcome or the byproduct of effort (Holloway, 1988). Which belief educators subscribe to has a significant impact on the expectations they hold for their students. The belief that student achievement is the visible manifestation of something that is fixed and unalterable provides educators with a failsafe excuse when some students don't succeed. These educators can safely say that those students who didn't succeed lacked the required ability, and as educators, there was little that they could do.

The fixed intelligence mindset can be exhibited in some interesting ways. For example, a small school district, in an effort to recruit students through the schools-of-choice program, advertised its mission in the local newspapers. The district leaders declared that their mission was "to educate all children to their fullest potential." Parents interested in doing whatever they could to ensure the best possible education for their children would certainly want to learn more about the school district's offerings.

Unfortunately, everyone has had experiences in which something turns out to be different from what was originally presented. The district whose mission was to educate all students to their fullest potential is one such case. The first question a parent should ask of this district is, "What conclusion do you come to if my child or any other child is not educationally successful?" Given the district's stated mission, the leaders have an "out" if a child is not successful—to say (or at least believe) that the unsuccessful student lacked potential. Do you think this school district would be prepared to offer a money-back guarantee if the parents felt the school district did not educate their children to their fullest potential? Do you know of any educators who can honestly say they have educated students to their fullest potential? Probably not.

Another story illustrates how the concept of ability can cloud one's vision when it comes to expectations and the successful education of all children. A few years ago, a middle school principal asked her consultant to meet individually with a teacher who was having difficulty coming to terms with the learning-for-all concept. The teacher was absolutely convinced that expectations for student performance had to be conditioned by a student's cognitive ability. Before attempting to answer the teacher's concern, the consultant asked her two questions. The first question was, "As a teacher, what conclusion do you draw if a student's cognitive ability score is much higher than his observed achievement would indicate?" The teacher said she would conclude that the student was not working up to her potential. The consultant then asked, "What conclusion do you draw if you find that a student's cognitive ability score is actually lower than her achievement would indicate?" The teacher said that she would question the validity of either the test or the indicators of achievement. The consultant suggested to her that educators are not allowed to have it both ways. It is unfair to draw one conclusion when the data conform to their concept of ability and reject the data when they don't confirm their expectations and beliefs.

The Expectations Elephant in the Room

The single most accurate indicator on which individual and organizational expectations turn in public schools is poverty. You can test this for yourself by using the following example. Describe two schools to a group of educators, and see how they react. Describe the first school as one where the student population comes mostly from middle-class homes and neighborhoods, and where parents are employed in middle-class careers and are socially and financially stable. Then ask the educators for a show of hands as to how many of them believe that the assessed achievement in the school is above the 60th percentile on a standardized test. You'll see most hands go up. Describe the second school as one with a transient student population coming from mostly single-parent homes with limited economic resources and a neighborhood in decline. Now ask the educators how many believe that the measured achievement in this school is below the 40th percentile on the same test. Again, you'll probably see most of them raise their hands. The significant point is that most educators form their impressions and expectations based on who goes to the school. In these examples, nothing was said about what happens in each school, only who attends.

Larry Lezotte recalls a story that illustrates this point based on a real situation that occurred in Prince Georges County, Maryland, a number of years ago. The two schools in the example were College Park Elementary School, where students mostly came from families associated with the University of Maryland, and Columbia Park Elementary School, located in an impoverished area near the District of Columbia. Shockingly, many people just could not accept that the middle-class students scored at the 90th percentile on average, while the poor children scored at the 94th percentile! This example should cause us to pause and reflect on a famous quote by Ron Edmonds:

> How many effective schools would you have to see to be persuaded of the educability of poor children? If your answer is more than one, then I submit that you have reasons of your own for preferring to believe that basic pupil performance derives from family background instead of school response to family background. (1979, p. 24)

Since Edmonds made that statement, effective schools research has consistently provided evidence that counters assumptions that family background is the primary determinant of student achievement. Yet the critical question remains: are educators any closer to letting go of the assumption that poverty equals low achievement? The perceived (assumed causal) relationship between student background and student achievement becomes real when it shapes the expectations of individual teachers and whole-school cultures. Because of the accident of geography, schools do tend to be judged by who attends: poor children tend to be clustered together, as do middle-class children. As a result of the expectations phenomena, schools tend to become known as high- or low-achieving schools independent of the quality of the curriculum and instructional program offered. However, educators can overcome the negative expectations phenomenon by implementing the correlate of high expectations for success and committing themselves to the learning-for-all mission.

High Expectations in Action

Expectations are personal beliefs we hold in our in our heads and hearts. Unfortunately, expectations, though personal, are not private. They influence our day-to-day behavior. In schools, the expectations held by the principals and teachers have a significant impact on the learners and learning by setting the learning climate of the school and its classrooms.

High Expectations and Leadership

High expectations are judged not only by the staff's initial beliefs and behaviors, but also by the organization's (and by association, the leader's) response when some students do not learn. Consider the situation in which a teacher plans and delivers a lesson, finds that some students did not learn to proficiency, but still goes on to teach the next lesson. The teacher's decision to proceed with the next lesson indicates that he didn't expect those particular students to learn in the first place. If the school leader, through silence, condoned that teacher's behavior, then that leader apparently held the same expectation as the teacher—she did not expect these students to learn or the teacher to teach them.

Leaders must help transform their schools, as cultural organizations, from teacher-centered institutions to learner-centered organizations in which teachers have high expectations of themselves as professionals, and have access to appropriate resources to help them ensure that every child learns. Leaders have to help their colleagues overcome the often-ingrained belief that some students simply can't be reached. Strong principals make it their mission to eliminate the pervasive willingness on the part of the faculty to write off some students as lost and unworthy of continued effort (Mero, Hartzman, & Boone, 2005a).

Many studies have shown that the principal's leadership impacts the climate and culture of the school and indirectly affects student learning. Principals have a primary responsibility to work with their staff to develop a culture that promotes and encourages student learning. They have the ability to shape the values, beliefs, and attitudes that are necessary to promote a stable and nurturing learning environment that in turn positively impacts student performance (MacNeil, Prater, & Busch, 2009). These leaders consistently and stubbornly reinforce a culture of high expectations, through both word and deed.

Teacher Behavior

In several studies, teacher expectations have been shown to relate to student achievement (Cawelti, 1999; Cotton, 2000; Hoover-Dempsey, Bassler, & Brissie, 1987). These studies provide insights into the subtle and not-so-subtle ways in which teachers convey (intentionally or unintentionally) different expectations to different students in their classrooms. Understanding those behaviors that convey high versus low expectations to students is the purpose of Teacher Expectations and Student Achievement (TESA), a staff development program offered through the Los Angeles County Office of Education. This program focuses on fifteen teacher behaviors proven to convey expectations to students. Some of the teacher behaviors taught in the program include such classroom routines as who gets called upon by the teacher and how frequently, which students receive the most detailed feedback on written work, and how long the teacher waits for students to come up with answers to questions. The interactions related to teacher expectations and student achievement are described in the accompanying chart in table 3.1 (page 46).

Practitioner Perspectives and Insights

Staff participation is critical to the successful implementation of the correlates. The online surveys that we have conducted provide valuable insights into factors that enable a staff to use the correlates to build and sustain an effective school. In January 2009, we conducted an online Reality Check survey focused on the high expectations for success correlate. The survey contained questions about key aspects of the correlate:

- Personal beliefs about the ability of all children to learn

- Observations about colleagues' expectations for all students

- Effect of the standards and accountability movement on expectations for student success

- Perceptions of teachers' and administrators' sense of efficacy

- Effect of school or district policies, procedures, and structures on expectations

- Strategies that have been useful in raising and maintaining high expectations for success

A total of 413 educators responded to the survey; 46 percent of the respondents associated themselves with elementary schools, 29 percent were associated with middle schools and senior high schools, and the remaining 25 percent were from other settings, mostly central office.

Nearly 91 percent of respondents indicated they personally believed that all children, regardless of race, ethnicity, or poverty level, can learn to a proficient level. Eighty-seven respondents (21 percent) offered a qualifying comment, most of which indicated that students with special needs are not likely to learn to a level of proficiency unless there are significant changes in the delivery system. In other words, these educators are saying, "We believe that the vast majority can learn to a proficient level, but not unless more time, more supports, and greater customization options are available." Simply put: practitioners believe the system needs to change.

Table 3.1: Teacher Expectations and Student Achievement—Fifteen Teacher Behaviors for Success

In TESA workshops, teachers learn the following interactions:	
Equitable Distribution of Response Opportunity	The teacher learns how to provide an opportunity for all students to respond or perform in classroom learning situations.
Affirmation or Correction	The teacher learns how to give feedback to students about their classroom performance.
Proximity	The teacher learns the significance of being physically close to students as they work.
Individual Helping	The teacher learns how to provide individual help to each student.
Praise for the Learning Performance	The teacher learns how to praise the students' learning performance.
Courtesy	The teacher learns how to use expressions of courtesy in interactions with students.
Latency	The teacher learns how to allow the student enough time to think over a question before assisting the student or ending the opportunity to respond.
Reasons for Praise	The teacher learns how to give useful feedback for the students' learning performance.
Personal Interest Statements and Compliments	The teacher learns how to ask questions, give compliments, or make statements related to a student's personal interests or experiences.
Delving, Rephrasing, Giving Clues	The teacher learns how to provide additional information to help the student respond to a question.
Listening	The teacher learns how to apply active listening techniques with students.
Touching	The teacher learns how to touch students in a respectful, appropriate, and friendly manner.
Higher-Level Questioning	The teacher learns how to ask challenging questions that require students to do more than simply recall information.
Accepting Feelings	The teacher learns how to recognize and accept students' feelings in a nonevaluative manner.
Desisting	The teacher learns how to stop a student's misbehavior in a calm and courteous manner.

When asked to estimate what percentage of staff hold high expectations for all students, 62 percent indicated that more than 75 percent of the staff members have high expectations for all. Twenty-seven percent indicated that they believed that more than 90 percent held high expectations for all students.

Respondents were then asked whether the standards, assessment, and accountability had increased, decreased, or left unchanged staff expectations for student success grounded in the learning-for-all mission. Seventy-four percent (299 respondents) indicated that they perceived that expectations had increased, while 19 percent perceived that expectations had not changed. Fifteen respondents believed that more administrators had higher expectations, but that the number of teachers with high expectations was unchanged.

The second section of the online survey asked respondents to share their perceptions of teacher and administrator sense of efficacy. Efficacy was defined as the belief that individuals can successfully accomplish what is being asked of them. A little over half (57 percent) believed that 75 percent of the teachers had a high and positive sense of efficacy. On the other hand, 43 percent perceived that less than 75 percent of the staff had a high sense of efficacy. When asked to rate the sense of efficacy of the school principals they knew, most (64 percent) indicated that more than 75 percent of the principals they knew had a high sense of efficacy. Approximately 25 percent indicated that 51–75 percent of the principals had a high sense of efficacy, while 10 percent indicated that 50 percent or fewer had a high sense of efficacy.

The respondents were asked to indicate the extent to which the school *as a whole* reflected a high sense of efficacy when it came to the school's ability to accomplish the learning-for-all mission. Sixty-two percent believed that the school's sense of efficacy was high or very high, while 32 percent rated the school's sense of efficacy to be average; only 6 percent rated their school's sense of efficacy as low or very low.

Respondents were asked to agree or disagree with the following statement: "Current school and/or district policies, procedures, and structures encourage high expectations for all students." Sixty-two percent agreed or strongly agreed with the statement, and 22 percent were uncertain or disagreed with it.

Let's summarize what the respondents seemed to be saying:

1. Almost all educators (90 percent) believe that nearly all students can learn to a proficient level.

2. Most teachers believe that they can successfully do what is being asked of them.

3. Nearly all administrators and the vast majority of schools have a high sense of efficacy.

4. School district policies, practices, and programs do not interfere with the learning-for-all mission.

These responses leave us with as many questions as we set out to answer. The big question that the responses raise is this: if we take these educators' views at face value, why aren't more schools, teachers, and students being more successful when success is defined as learning to a level of proficiency?

Research-Supported Strategies

In our review of research related to school improvement, we identified studies that provide evidence that high expectations for success produce positive results for all students. Examples of these studies include the following.

Believe that all children can succeed. A program called *Success for All®* was built on the idea that every child can and must succeed in reading. The program starts with top-quality curricula and instruction. Struggling readers receive tutoring as necessary, different approaches to reading instruction, help getting eyeglasses if needed, or help with behavioral or attendance problems. Help is given early and until the student succeeds (Slavin et al., 1996).

Use data to inform instruction. In 1995, the Kennewick Public Schools in Kennewick, Washington, began to measure students' growth at the beginning and end of a school year from third through tenth grade. Using data to inform instruction resulted in a different mindset for teachers, administrators, parents, and the community. The all-or-nothing approach gave way to more frequent assessing, which provided more timely feedback to adjust instruction, reteach, and focus on learning deficits. Assessment, therefore, became integrated into the teaching-and-learning process (Fielding, Kerr, & Rosier, 2007).

De-track the curriculum. The Rockville Centre High School in Long Island, New York, not only de-tracked the curriculum, but also made the eleventh- and twelfth-grade International Baccalaureate® (IB) curriculum, previously reserved for gifted and talented students, available to every student. To help students prepare, staff created a new preparatory curriculum for ninth and tenth graders and de-tracked classes in sixth to eighth grades. While not required, participation in the IB program by minority students increased from just a handful to over 50 percent, and the performance gap on the New York Regents Exam all but disappeared (Garrity & Burris, 2007).

Develop personalized intervention plans. Velasquez Elementary in Richmond, Texas, is made up of around six hundred students, over 50 percent of whom qualify for free and reduced-price lunch, 67 percent of whom are minority and 16 percent of whom are limited English proficient (LEP). The teachers have a non-negotiable commitment to the learning-for-all concept. Staff members meet as a core team on a weekly basis to disaggregate data and identify students who need help. They then create and deliver a personalized intervention plan. This process produced admirable results (Berkey & Dow, 2008).

Don't accept failure. At Bendle Middle School in Burton, Michigan, staff required students to complete every assignment to high standards. Students were required to achieve at least a C on every assignment. If the work was less than C quality, the student received an I for incomplete. Teachers then gave students the time and support to complete the work and get a higher grade (Kenkel, Hoelscher, & West, 2006).

Developing a Data Dashboard

To maintain a successful program of school improvement, administrators and teachers must participate in activities that monitor progress in the application of the correlates. Data collected through perceptual surveys, self reports, and third-party direct observations can help identify indicators of the effectiveness of teaching and learning in the school or district.

Perceptual Survey Questions

These types of questions can be used to ascertain the degree to which the correlate of high expectations for success is present and functioning in the school or district. Ask respondents to indicate their level of agreement (strongly agree, agree, undecided, disagree, strongly disagree, or not applicable) regarding statements such as:

- The school's policies, practices, and behavior reflect high expectations for all students.

- Generally, teachers in your school do not believe that they have the skills and knowledge necessary to ensure that nearly all the students in their classes master the intended curriculum.

- As a teacher, I make sure my students master the skills being taught before I proceed to the next learning task.

Self-Report Questions

These questions are examples that fit this correlate:

- Were there any students this past week whose academic progress fell below your expectations for them? If yes, did you inform the student and his or her parents?

- Were there any students this past week whose academic progress exceeded your expectations for them? If yes, did you inform the student and his or her parents?

- Based on your knowledge of the students so far this year, are there any students who are likely to not master the intended curriculum in your class (grade) this year?

Students to whom teachers refer in responding to these questions should be named so that specific concerns about their performance can be addressed. Although it is necessary for researchers to omit the names of individuals to honor anonymity, this condition does not apply in a school where the staff is implementing the correlate of high expectations for success. To ensure student success, teachers and administrators need to know who to help, when, and how.

Third-Party Direct Observations

A great deal of the research on teacher expectations has taken the form of direct observation by a researcher who generally is not part of the class community. While the observer does not have to be a researcher, the individual should be trained on the observation scheme to be used. Some examples of observational variables are listed below. These examples are adapted from the Teacher Expectations and Student Achievement program referred to earlier in the chapter:

- Does the teacher distribute question-asking and turn-taking evenly across all students in the class?

- When a teacher calls upon a student, does he or she provide equal and adequate wait time for each student to formulate an answer?

- What percent of the students are actively engaged in doing what the teacher has requested during repeated three-minute scans of activities in the classroom?

Data collected through third-party direct observations should offer objective evidence about what happens in the classroom in various circumstances. If these data are to provide evidence of growth in implementing the correlate, the same tools should be used to ensure consistency and validity.

Conclusion

The high expectations for success correlate is both elusive and pervasive. It is elusive because so much of its influence is carried in the staff's beliefs and values. It is nearly impossible and often dangerous to pretend that we can look into the heart of the teachers and administrators and draw conclusions about their beliefs. The correlate is pervasive in the sense that staff expectations for individual students and groups of students can be as subtle as teachers calling on students during class, or as overt as placing students in tracks that virtually ensure that some are doomed to a less-challenging curriculum. Student placements in courses of study can work like the self-fulfilling prophecy: staff didn't believe that these students could learn, and sure enough, they didn't learn! How reassuring to know that the decision was proven correct.

Achieving this correlate is critical to the discussion of effective schools because individuals and organizations are always moving in the direction of their beliefs. If educators believe that some students can't and won't learn, negative outcomes are likely to result. On the other hand, if educators believe that all students can and will learn, positive outcomes are likely to be achieved.

CHAPTER 4

Strong Instructional Leadership

In the effective school, the principal acts as an instructional leader by persistently communicating the mission to the staff, students, parents, and larger community. The principal understands the principles of effective instruction and uses that knowledge in the management of the instructional program.

Like any organization, schools are perfectly aligned to continue to get the same results over time. If the current results fulfill the school's mission, the staff does not need to change what they are doing. The staff members need only to do what they have been doing and they are likely to get what they have been getting all along—mission accomplished! In such a fortuitous situation (assuming, of course, that all is well in terms of student learning), the organization can function with an effective manager of the status quo, someone who works to maintain the organization's current effectiveness, perhaps doing so even more efficiently.

On the other hand, if the school's mission changes (and we know that it has), a manager of the status quo is not enough. The organization needs an individual who will be an effective leader—a leader who can create commitment and buy-in to the new mission and help the staff change tactics, strategies, and behaviors to advance the organization toward the new mission. Schools must now—and for the foreseeable future—focus on leadership and cannot be satisfied only with effective management. This is borne out by the effective schools research that has consistently found that effective schools have strong and effective leadership.

The school principal, as the instructional leader, has an especially important obligation to create a shared understanding and commitment to the mission. Further, it falls particularly to the leadership to keep the focus on the mission. We find that the leaders in effective schools depend on proactive, interactive, and reactive strategies to ensure the mission remains the center of attention.

This correlate also makes clear that the principal must be a well-informed student of teaching and learning. Unfortunately, typical administrator preparation programs that credential individuals for the principalship have not emphasized mastery of teaching and learning, curriculum, and instruction knowledge bases. This observation should not be interpreted to mean that all school leaders lack adequate knowledge of the technical core of the school's work. Rather, our experience has shown that, either by design or by chance, leaders in the effective schools are better prepared in these critical areas.

Although the principal is expected to be, and usually is, the instructional leader, we have found effective schools where there is strong instructional leadership, but the principal is *not* the instructional leader. Sometimes the instructional leadership falls to an assistant principal, lead teacher, or someone else who commands the respect of the staff and is afforded the authority to lead. Make no mistake, the person who is being paid to be the school leader—the principal—*should* be the instructional leader. But sometimes, for many reasons, someone other than the principal provides the necessary leadership to ensure school effectiveness.

The correlate description reads as though the needed instructional leadership can only come from an individual. This is typically the case. However, efforts to create collaborative school leadership teams have produced an emerging collaborative leadership model. With this model, a collaborative team (which may or may not include the principal) serves as the source of instructional leadership. No matter what form it takes, instructional leadership is a nonnegotiable for schools to be effective.

Learning to Lead

"Born leader" is a description often attributed to an individual who excels in leading or working effectively with others. However, leadership is not something that is innate and inborn, although like any skill, it comes easier to some than others. Nor is it a product of personality or charisma. Leadership arises from the effective use of a specific set of skills and behaviors that can be learned, practiced, and refined. The effective leader not only is an expert in using these skills and behaviors, but also is able to adapt them to the organizational context within which he or she works.

Many books on educational leadership are readily available (see, for example, Blankstein, Houston, & Cole, 2009; Marzano & Waters, 2009; Reason, 2010; and Reeves, 2006). Such resources can assist aspiring leaders and veteran leaders to become more effective in leadership roles. We explored the leadership concept more fully within the context of continuous school improvement in a previous book, *Stepping Up: Leading the Charge to Improve Our Schools,* so we won't attempt to duplicate that text here (Lezotte & McKee, 2006). Instead, we present some of the key concepts of strong instructional leadership.

Leadership and Authority

Leadership is often confused with authority, but in fact they are very different concepts. For example, the superintendent can give you the *authority* to be the principal of a school, but she can't make you the instructional *leader*, no matter how much authority she bestows. Whether you become the leader of your school depends on the staff, parents, and students of your school; they must *choose* you to be their leader. This important insight is one that many individuals entering the role of principal or superintendent miss, to their detriment. Given this insight, we define leadership as follows: *Leadership (whether from an individual or a team) is the ability to take a "followership" to a place they have never been and are not sure they want to go.*

Several elements in this definition deserve further comment. According to our definition, leadership is about change. The focus on change is what separates leaders from managers. Generally, managers are responsible and accountable for deploying current available resources, human and material, in a manner that efficiently contributes to the mission. While functioning as managers, individuals are not generally expected to be the champions of change. On the other hand, leaders, even in roles typically reserved for managers, are seen (and see themselves) as "change agents." The emphasis on and search for effective leaders, as opposed to good managers, appears whenever an institution or organization is under pressure to change or to be replaced. Today, education is at a point where many feel that public schools must either change or be replaced. Public education needs effective leadership today, perhaps more so than at any other time in its history.

Leaders will not be effective if they simply try to command change. They must develop and maintain a followership. One cannot claim leader status if no one is willing to join the journey. To be effective change agents who are embraced by would-be followers, leaders must be able to do two things: communicate a clear and compelling vision of where they are attempting to take their organizations and why, and establish a trusting relationship with their followers. Trust is critical between the leader and the followers since, as we state in our working definition, they are "not sure they want to go." Change represents risk to most people. Even if the followers are convinced that the vision is compelling, they won't be comfortable committing to the change unless they can count on the leader to support them in the necessary processes. This support will come in part through the provision of new knowledge and skills, along with a safe, encouraging environment to test out those skills. Such support will enable the followers to effectively implement the intended changes. In this context, leading and teaching should be thought of as two sides of the same coin. Effective leaders are effective teachers.

The interplay between effective leading through effective teaching is especially true in education. The men and women who staff the schools see themselves as professionals. Being a professional means, among other things, that one has a relatively high degree of independence in conducting one's work. In addition, professionals continue to learn and grow with the profession itself. To do so, they must have a process that is based on both new learning and ongoing support.

Leadership Qualities

James Kouzes and Barry Posner (1987), authors of *The Leadership Challenge*, have conducted years of research focusing on what followers look for in and expect from their leaders. They have identified four qualities that followers expect and rank-ordered the qualities from most important to least important.

1. **Trustworthiness:** Our definition of leadership indicates that the leader is seeking to take the followers to "a place they have never been and are not sure they want to go." This unknown place represents significant change that may seem, to the followers, idealistic, abstract, perhaps unreachable or even frightening. To overcome resistance to change, leaders must earn the trust and confidence of those being asked to change.

   Simply said, followers expect leaders to say what they mean and mean what they say. Followers need to feel that they can depend on leaders to act consistently with what they say—leaders have to "walk the talk." It may take a while for followers to trust new leaders, but each time the leaders are perceived as acting consistently with the organization's mission and their expressed vision, the followers' trust grows. Unfortunately, while it takes time to develop trust, it only takes one or two breaches of that trust to destroy it completely. Once trust is lost, leaders will have a next-to-impossible challenge to regain it.

2. **Competence:** Followers expect leaders to know what they're doing and bring a repertoire of knowledge and skills to the organization. As noted in the definition of the strong instructional leadership correlate, effective instructional leaders must "understand the principles of effective instruction and use that knowledge in the management of the instructional program." However, this statement doesn't mean that leaders must be experts in every area. It does mean that leaders need to know what they know, what they don't know, who *does* know, and how to get the necessary knowledge.

   To that end, it's important that school leaders have a strong sense of efficacy about effective instruction, and be prepared to listen to and support other staff who have strengths in areas needed for school effectiveness. School leaders must model an authentic image of a learner. By doing so, they demonstrate confidence in the continuous improvement process.

3. **Forward-looking:** The attribute of being "forward-looking" simply means being able to choose an appropriate direction for the organization. According to Kouzes and Posner, "Followers ask that a leader have a well-defined orientation toward the future. We want to know what the company will look like, feel like, be like when it arrives at its goal in six months or six years" (1987, p. 20).

Even though the amount of work to be done in the here and now is overwhelming, effective leaders spend a significant amount of their time and effort focused about six months or more in the future. Effective leaders have the ability to anticipate the future and are prepared to guide the followership to and through the expected and unexpected "turns in the road." They are constantly examining new research, best practices, and new systems to find ways to make their organization more effective. Effective leaders embrace a continuous improvement mindset and establish and nurture that mindset among the followers.

4. **Enthusiasm:** Followers expect their leaders to project a spirit of optimism and excitement about the school, its mission, and prospects for the future. Given the many challenges facing schools every day (for example, finances, student discipline, and teacher morale), it is very easy for leaders to become discouraged and project that to the staff and other stakeholders. Here is an example of the difficulty that school leaders face.

Imagine that, as the school leader, you have just spent a significant chunk of time wading through a serious personnel, student, or budget problem. You leave your office to go down the hall for a drink of water. You run into a colleague who asks, "How's it going?" If you want to create and maintain a spirit of enthusiasm, you'll have to respond, "It's going great! Can't wait until tomorrow. It will be even better!" On the other hand, to see the positive energy leave the organization, all you would have to do is suggest that the colleague take a seat and get comfortable, so that you can talk about just how bad things are going. It may be difficult for the leader to muster enthusiasm on any given day, but never underestimate the positive difference enthusiasm can make when it comes to inspiring the followership in an organization.

Leadership Style and Sustainable Change

Approaches to change have evolved and these approaches have in turn influenced thinking about leadership style. In his book *Terms of Engagement: Changing the Way We Change Organizations*, Richard Axelrod (2002) describes a paradigm that he and his colleagues have found to be particularly effective in promoting sustainable change. His engagement paradigm is based on four key principles:

1. Widening the circle of involvement

2. Creating communities for action

3. Connecting people to each other

4. Embracing democracy

The engagement paradigm requires a dramatically different approach to leadership. Widening the circle of involvement involves a willingness to reach out to individuals with varied knowledge and skills; this action requires patience and persistence. Creating communities for action and allowing people to connect with one another and with a compelling purpose demonstrate the leader's level of self-confidence and willingness to trust others.

These actions may seem risky to leaders who fear that doing so will allow the resisters to get organized and powerful. However, resisters often lack a singularity of purpose that detracts from their ability to overcome the positive effects of a wider circle of involvement and communities of action. Embracing democratic principles means sharing control. Applying this principle can be particularly challenging for individuals who are accustomed to the command-and-control structure common in bureaucracy, and for those who believe control and leadership are synonymous.

Thomas Sergiovanni (1989) identifies two approaches to leadership:

1. *Transactional leadership* is the more traditional view, with an emphasis on rules, procedures, and job descriptions to accomplish goals and objectives.

2. *Transformational leadership* relies on shared purpose, beliefs and values, empowerment, and team orientation.

Both types of leadership have their uses, and effective leaders learn to adapt their leadership styles over time, with the goal of inspiring and empowering colleagues to take ownership of the change process in pursuit of a common vision. These concepts are illustrated in figure 4.1, which shows how effective leaders evolve in their leadership styles as their organizations move from groups of autonomous individuals to collaborative learning communities committed to the learning-for-all mission.

The work of Sergiovanni (1989) and Axelrod (2002) provides the framework for expanding the goal of instructional leadership to encompass all adults related to the school (and especially the teachers).

The role of principal becomes a leader of leaders, rather than a leader of followers. The leader's greatest contribution to the school or district community is to articulate a vision to which all stakeholders can commit and to create a community of shared values guided by the "magnetic north" of the mission. This broader concept of leadership recognizes our previous premise that leadership is always delegated from the followership, and that expertise is generally distributed among many, not concentrated in a single person.

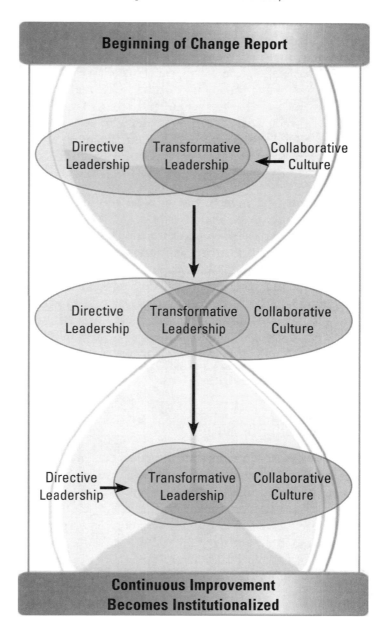

Figure 4.1: The evolution of leadership in a changing organization.

Leaders Must Be Students of History

Even in the face of compelling calls for change, educational leaders have had difficulty responding. Often this is because they underestimate the organization's history and the power that history has on the way schools operate today.

Schools have had a difficult time freeing themselves from their early history when the one-room schoolhouse was the prevailing image of a school. As schools evolved into larger structures with many rooms, the outer appearance of the building changed, but the basic operations of an individual classroom remained largely an autonomous unit under the jurisdiction of the individual teacher. Really, the only difference between the one-room school and today's larger buildings is that autonomous classrooms now share a common wall with each other. Or, as Eaker so wittily remarked, "The traditional school often functions as a collection of independent contractors united by a common parking lot" (as cited in Schmoker, 2006, p. 23).

Effective leaders must be prepared to address the independent contractor mindset to meet the challenge of change in a school or district. For example, assume that the teachers hold the view that the school should function in the way that Eaker ironically described. Further, assume that those teachers relish their independence. How do you think these teachers will perceive the role and responsibilities of the school's principal? They may suggest that the primary role and responsibility of the principal is to keep the halls clear so it's easy to get from the parking lot to the classrooms. On the other hand, assume that the teachers hold the view that a school is a complex, goal-oriented, resource-limited, people-driven social system. With regard to teachers who ascribe to this mental model, we would expect their views to produce a very different set of expectations for the role of the principal.

Instructional Leadership in Action

An effective leader is able to put into practice the qualities and behaviors described in the previous sections of this chapter. Are such leaders in today's schools? Do teachers have confidence and trust in their leaders? What needs to happen to ensure that instructional leadership is effective? These questions are representative of those we asked in our instructional leadership Reality Check online survey conducted in the spring of 2009. Like the survey conducted on high expectations for success, we received many responses that presented perspectives and insights from practitioners representing all levels of teaching, as well as other educational roles.

Practitioner Perspectives and Insights

A total of 411 educators responded to the instructional leadership survey. Of these, 43 percent of the respondents associated themselves with the elementary level, 31 percent were associated primarily with the intermediate and secondary level, and the remaining 26 percent were associated with other roles, mostly with the central office. With the demand for school reform that most schools are facing, it is generally agreed that school leaders must be effective change agents if schools are to successfully meet the challenges of reform. With that as the context, the survey asked the respondents to indicate the percentage of current school leaders they considered to be effective change leaders. Nearly two-thirds (64 percent) indicated that only about half of the leaders were ready and able to lead change. These results are very unsettling for those committed to the correlate of strong instructional leadership as an essential element of sustainable school reform.

In the survey, the respondents were asked to indicate the percentage of school leaders who are prepared to lead the systemic changes necessary for sustainable school improvement. A majority (58 percent) indicated the school leaders were "well" or "somewhat" prepared for the systemic challenge. To the contrary, 39 percent indicated that their current school leaders were generally not adequately prepared or not prepared at all.

Various projections report that a large percentage of current school leaders will reach retirement age in the next five years. These vacancies present both opportunity and challenge. An item in the survey asked respondents to indicate how confident they felt that public schools would have an adequate pool of qualified leaders from which to choose replacements for retiring principals and superintendents. A slight majority (51 percent) indicated that they had little or no confidence that strong and qualified candidates would be available.

In general, the respondents' perceptions regarding current and future school leaders paint a rather gloomy picture. If these educators' perceptions are accurate, the future of educational leadership needs immediate attention and decisive action. To continue what we have been doing and employing individuals who are not ready to lead change (especially systemic change) means that the pace of school reform will never reach escape velocity from the status quo.

Trust Them, Trust Them Not

As evidenced by Kouzes and Posner's (1987) work cited earlier, trust in the leader is the cornerstone of effective and sustainable leadership and change. Yet when asked in our survey, teachers and other school staff expressed reservations regarding the level of trust they had in school leaders, especially principals. When asked what, in their experience, tended to undermine trust in school leaders, a total of 395 individuals offered a wide range of responses.

Poor communication was the single most frequently cited factor undermining the respondents' trust in their leaders. Many respondents felt that school leaders did not communicate clear policies and expectations, and failed to share their vision and values with the staff. In addition, respondents reported that trust was often undermined because the school leaders did not involve staff in decision making, they didn't seem to believe in the teachers, they lacked empathy, and they failed to provide support. Finally, many respondents said that trust suffered when the school leaders said one thing and did another, failed to follow through, and generally lacked consistency.

Is the School Leader's Job Doable?

Some researchers (Bennis, 1989; Bowsher, 2003) have argued that the school leader's role has expanded so much over the last couple of decades that it is unrealistic to believe that one person can effectively do all that the role currently demands. In our survey, we asked practitioners to share their perspectives on whether the position is too complex and overloaded for one person to fulfill effectively. The responses from 396 of those participating in the survey indicated that respondents were divided in their views of the "doability" of the leadership function. About half of the respondents expressed the view that the job had become overloaded with more and more duties, with responsibilities being added every day. The other half felt that the job was doable and that those who didn't share that view either needed to get out the leadership role or shouldn't have gone into it in the first place.

However, even the half who expressed the view that the school leader role is indeed doable said that it can only be done successfully by high-energy, well-organized individuals, skilled in and comfortable with delegating responsibilities to others.

The Pace of School Reform

Finally, practitioners were asked if the slower-than-desired pace of school reform could be attributed to a lack of effective instructional leadership. Of the 411 respondents, 45 percent said no, that the slower-than-desired pace was not attributable to a lack of leadership, while 47 percent indicated that the lack of school leadership was at least a significant contributor to the slower pace.

Leadership Preparation and Strategies

We asked practitioners what changes they would recommend for school leadership preparation programs. Three hundred and eighty-five individuals offered a wide variety of suggestions. Some higher-frequency patterns emerged:

- Focus training less on theory and more on applied, real-world courses and experiences.

- Include more courses to ensure that future school leaders have a deeper understanding of curriculum and instruction and the leader's role.

- Provide training that gives the candidates the knowledge base on how to develop collaboration, build teams, and coach staff, all of which are especially needed to ensure teacher development.

- Require future school leaders to participate in internships and apprenticeships prior to assuming the leader role, activities similar to student teaching.

- Change the organizational structure to provide school leaders with an administrative assistant for the paperwork and other routine tasks, thus freeing the principal to actually engage in required leader behaviors.

Many respondents went on to say that leaders can be successful only if they get their priorities right and are able to strike a balance between the managerial and leadership tasks. A few suggested that the best solution might be to officially and formally divide the role into two parts (management and instructional leadership).

When asked to indicate what they thought school leaders should emphasize in their day-to-day routines, 393 practitioners offered diverse suggestions. The one that received the most support was that of conducting more classroom observations while focusing on curricular standards and using coaching strategies. A second grouping of suggestions focused on emphasizing formative assessments, examining and interpreting data, protecting instructional time, and removing bureaucratic barriers and challenges to teaching and learning. Many of the respondents wanted to see school leaders more active in facilitating collaborative discussions like those that are basic to professional learning communities and continuous school improvement.

When asked whether they had found strategies or programs that were effective in attracting and maintaining effective school leaders, 363 people responded. Few respondents identified formal programs that they had found to be effective. On the other hand, many of the respondents suggested district strategies that proved to be beneficial.

One strategy that was cited very often was to encourage school leaders to form collaborative groups in order to learn together and support one another. Several of the respondents reported that their districts have had success by formally and officially deciding to "grow their own school leaders." Another common suggestion was for school district boards and superintendents to strike the proper balance between micromanaging school leaders and communicating that the school leaders are on their own. School leaders need to feel that they can generally count on the superintendent and central office for support.

Research-Supported Strategies

From our review of research related to instructional leadership, we have selected several studies that define the leadership qualities and abilities required to build and maintain an effective school.

Articulate a vision. Public Agenda (2007) found that effective principals had an explicit vision of what their school could be and brought a can-do attitude to the job. Deal and Peterson (1999) called these individuals visionaries who develop a clear sense of the hopes and dreams of the school and communicate this positive image in powerful ways through ceremonies, stories, and language. In one school, Booher-Jennings (2005) found that forcing change without a shared vision and sense of mission created a climate of competition that undermined collegiality, making it almost impossible for the staff to work together. In this study, the lack of shared vision had adverse effects on efforts to improve instruction for the lowest scoring students on the state standardized test.

Use data. In Creighton's 2001 article "Data Analysis and the Principalship," he wrote that instructional leadership and data-driven leadership are inseparable. Educational leaders must use data and data analyses both to communicate the vision of where they are trying to take the school, and as a means of monitoring progress toward the vision. Principals in a study by Halverson, Grigg, Prichett, and Thomas (2007) demonstrated new instructional leadership skills that included the knowledge and frameworks of external accountability integrated within traditional practices of internal accountability models. Principals were able to create a professional community characterized by a focus on making sense of student learning data while simultaneously reshaping, refining, and adapting practice and performance through continuous improvement—not just by complying with external accountability standards.

Structure a collaborative process. Marks and Pinty (2003) found that the most effective schools had a high degree of engagement and collaboration between teachers and principal. The case study of South Loop Elementary School in Chicago revealed that carefully designed structures, routines, expectations, and processes facilitated collaboration (Baccellieri, 2010). Teachers were at the core of the collaborative change process in this school. They participated in a continuous cycle of assessments, data analysis, and curriculum planning.

Focus on teaching and learning. Marks and Pinty (2003) also found that schools that had leaders who focused the conversation on curriculum, instruction, and assessment had higher pedagogical quality and student achievement. Briggs and Wohlstetter (2003) reinforced these findings, determining that struggling schools were more likely to focus their discussions on procedures, the distribution of power, and housekeeping issues instead of teaching and learning.

Set high expectations for success and monitor progress. Cawelti and Protheroe, in their review of six high-performing districts, found that the district leaders "developed and nurtured widely-shared beliefs about learning, including high expectations, and . . . provided a strong focus on results" (2001, p. 98). Anderson and Davenport (2002) described a case study of one Texas school district where a no-excuses mindset and a strong focus on results took the district from low performing to exemplary. Bossidy and Charan (2002) noted that effective leaders have the ability to hold people accountable and be firm with those who are not performing. A leader who accommodates individuals who cannot or will not meet the standards discourages those who do.

Developing a Data Dashboard

Like each correlate, the conceptual description of the strong instructional leadership correlate has to be placed in the specific context or setting. For example, the instructional leader behaviors that most influence student and school effectiveness in the elementary setting may be different from those that matter most in secondary schools. Likewise, leadership qualities have been examined from many different perspectives and theories. The various theories frame different contexts for assessing the quality or strength of leadership found in different settings.

The effective schools research has consistently found that effective schools have strong and effective leadership. More than thirty years ago Ron Edmonds, in conversation with Larry Lezotte, observed that we have found schools that had strong instructional leaders that were not yet effective (meaning that leadership is necessary but not sufficient), but we have never found an effective school that lacked strong instructional leadership. This statement is as true today as it was when it was first made.

For purposes of developing measures that can be used to develop a baseline and to monitor change over time in the leadership of a school, three vital domains of leadership should be measured and monitored. The first (and perhaps most important) leadership domain focuses on the leader's role in setting and supporting the vision and mission of the school. Second, the leader's ability to manage the disciplinary climate of the school is an area where teachers are quick to judge the quality of the leader's performance. Finally, but no less important, is the leader's ability to manage the mission through the allocation of resources, especially the allocation of the talents of individual staff members, and by determining how time is deployed.

Perceptual Survey Questions

The following items illustrate the kind of survey questions that could be incorporated into any survey completed by any stakeholder group. Ask respondents to indicate their level of agreement (strongly agree, agree, undecided, disagree, strongly disagree, or not applicable) regarding statements such as:

- The principal effectively communicates the mission to all the major school constituencies.
- The principal has established a strong instructional focus in the school.
- Teachers' efforts to maintain the disciplinary climate of the school are supported by the principal.
- Teachers can count on the principal to help with instructional concerns or problems.

Self-Report Questions

As part of the overall data-gathering system used to assess the strong instructional leadership correlate, the following self-report questions might be useful to develop a baseline for describing the leader's behavior and monitoring change over time:

- How many classroom observations of more than ten minutes' duration did the principal conduct during the past week?

- How many parent-teacher conferences did the principal attend during the past week?

- How much time (estimated in minutes) did the principal spend examining school performance data during the past week?

- How many students did the principal meet with the past week because of discipline problems?

Third-Party Direct Observations

There are various ways a third-party observer could help inform implementation of the instructional leadership correlate in the school:

- The third-party observer could shadow the principal throughout the day. The observer could focus on the frequency with which the principal makes proactive, reactive, and interactive comments, and exhibits actions to remind and reinforce the mission, beliefs, and values of the school.

- The third-party observer could sit in on meetings, conferences, and collaborative discussions focusing on the number and quality of instances when the principal uses questions (rather than statements) to guide the conversations.

- Finally, the third-party observer could look at those situations not related to the learning mission that seem to demand and consume a large amount of the leader's time. The feedback from such inquiry could be used to develop strategies that enable the principal to invest more time in the behaviors known to advance student learning.

Conclusion

The effective schools research and the school improvement model based on that research have always taken the view that the school is a complex system and the principal must function as an effective instructional leader, more like the conductor of the orchestra than a custodian of the halls. Even if we believe that each teacher is like a virtuoso musician, we still need a world-class conductor to create and sustain a world-class orchestra, and so it is with schools. The systems approach to leading learning in the schools demands effective leadership. Schools need leaders with a passion for the learning mission, an understanding of the traditions within schools, and the courage to confront the system.

CHAPTER 5

Clear and Focused Mission

In the effective school, the staff develops a clearly articulated mission focusing on successful learning for all students. Through collaboration, the staff forms a shared understanding of and commitment to instructional goals, priorities, assessment procedures, and accountability.

This correlate speaks directly to the intent of the school and its teachers. It is a statement of what your school community believes about the school, the nature of schooling itself, and the capacity of your students to learn. It is a statement of what values are important to the school community and the way individuals within the community are expected to treat one another. It is a statement of what business your school is about and what you intend it to become. It should be the focus of all your school's improvement efforts, the driving force behind positive change.

In most schools, the staff spends little (if any) time talking about the mission, core values, and core beliefs. Generally speaking, educators tend to make huge untested assumptions that all the adults working in a school have a common understanding of the mission and a shared set of core values and beliefs. In reality, administrators and teachers often only vaguely understand the school culture, its underlying core beliefs and values, and the organizational mission. Why is a shared sense of mission so important?

Consider this analogy: it is likely that most of us have seen the beer commercial that features four pairs of Clydesdale horses pulling a wagon through the winter snow. The scene clearly conveys the power of the eight horses as they pull the wagon. Now imagine that the pairs of horses are reorganized: one pair is hooked to the wagon facing east, the second pair is facing west, the third pair is facing north, and the fourth pair is facing south. What's going to happen when the driver says, "Giddy up"? With this strange configuration, the team will go nowhere even though the same potential "horsepower" is available. Maximum output from the team happens only when all the horses are pulling the wagon in the same direction. So it is with the members of the school community.

The accountability and standards movement, embodied by NCLB, has jump-started the change process in many schools. However, sustainable change will only come from the collective internal understanding and commitment of the educators and other stakeholders to a common mission, a moral imperative of learning for all. It is crucial, then, that the mission for the school is well defined and compelling.

Word Choice Makes a Big Difference

To ensure that everyone understands the mission, the intent must be clearly defined. Effective schools advocates have championed the mission: learning for all, whatever it takes. Short, to the point, and clear. Or is it? Let's start with the little word *all*. In the effective school, all equals all—not all except poor students, not all except special education students; all means every child. Every stakeholder—administrators, teachers, support staff, students, parents, and the community—must understand and accept this concept. Otherwise, failures can easily be excused and justified.

Now let's look at the learning portion of the phrase. Learning, not teaching, is the focus of this mission statement. Establishing learning as the focus will profoundly influence the actions of the school community.

In chapter 1 we discussed the twin policy pillars of public education, equity and quality. How these two terms are ordered and connected in a school's narrative makes a huge difference when it comes to implementing the mission. Here are some typical connections that educators offer:

- Quality *and* equity
- Quality *or* equity
- Equity *through* quality
- Quality *with* equity
- Equity *in* quality

We prefer the expression "equity in quality." This wording conveys the sense that schools must provide equal opportunities for all students to participate in the full range of quality programs the school provides. In our view, this expression is closest to the current mission of public education. It makes little sense to worry about equity in schools and classrooms where the instructional program and services fail to meet the standard of quality.

Avoiding Mission Drift

Tom Peters and Bob Waterman (1982) stated that big organizations, by virtue of their "bigness," are always subject to drift away from their mission and core values. They went on to define a big organization as any organization that employs more than four people. This being so, virtually every school qualifies as a big organization and is subject to *mission drift*. The challenge for the effective school is first to reach clarity and consensus on the mission, core values, and beliefs, and second, to develop ongoing processes that ensure that the school and its staff don't drift off in different directions. One strategy effective schools use to stave off mission drift is to periodically review and renew the organization's mission, values, and beliefs.

The Relationship Between Mission and Core Beliefs and Values

An individual's values and beliefs are the cornerstones of his or her world view. Beliefs center around what an individual thinks is true. Values are grounded in how one thinks the world should be, rather than assumptions about the way world is. For example, if you believe that all children can master the essential curriculum, then a core value based on that belief is that all children should have an equal opportunity to learn. As you compare what you believe should be to your assessment of what is, you identify areas of dissonance—the reality of a situation falls short of what you believe it should be. Dissonance often produces a sense of discomfort. The desire to address dissonance and relieve discomfort drives us to address the problem, and that becomes our mission: learning for all, whatever it takes! This succinct statement can become a motto for those in search of a focused, clearly defined mission for their school.

School Culture and Mission

In the effective school, a clear mission that focuses on student learning drives the culture. Jenkins, Louis, Walberg, and Keefe (1994) found that perhaps the most significant feature that "world-class schools" had in common was their continual effort toward becoming "learning organizations with a commitment to continuous problem-solving and a sense of shared responsibility for improvement" (p. 72). In their meta-analysis of research on disadvantaged schools that showed significant improvement in student outcomes, Muijas, Harris, Chapman, Stoll, and Russ (2004) reinforced this assertion. But make no mistake, school culture built around the learning-for-all mission is not just about feeling good about the organization. Rodriguez (2008) defined school culture as "what schools *do* and how they do [it]" (p. 761). He emphasized that adult behaviors are key to a culture of learning—particularly behaviors that are underscored by the *push factor*. The push factor is highlighted by those adult behaviors that challenge, stretch, and motivate students and convey a "you can do it" attitude. Clearly, in this setting mission and high expectations intersect.

The culture of a school represents a complex and powerful set of interdependent forces that function to ensure that the school does again tomorrow what it did today. As such, school culture can serve as a major source of resistance to change. The good news is that while the school culture is complex and powerful, only about 5 percent of an organization's culture is mission critical. That is to say, a few traits of the school culture are important, but most of them matter hardly at all. If school change efforts can remain focused on the mission-critical 5 percent, change will be more likely to be both successful and sustainable. How do you determine what is mission critical? Through the identification and clarification of the school's core beliefs and values. This will allow you to differentiate the vital few aspects of the culture that are critical to attaining the mission from those that make no difference.

The process of defining the mission involves identifying those beliefs, values, and goals necessary to achieve the mission. By centering attention on these factors, stakeholders have opportunities to clarify the mission—"what they expect students to learn, how they will know that students are learning, what they will do when students are not learning, and what they will do to ensure that all students receive the instruction they need" (Donelson & Donelson, 2010, p. 123). A well-defined mission shapes the culture of the school.

Courageous Mission Statements

The clear and focused mission correlate is integral to the concept of the effective school as a system. Recall this definition from chapter 2: the effective school is a system that is sustained through the interdependence of the learning-for-all mission, broad-based commitment to the mission, and strategies for monitoring the mission. Educators sometimes resist embracing the clear and focused mission correlate. These individuals, most likely, are fearful of making bold statements like "learning for all." They ask, "What will happen if we fall short of our stated mission?" Such remarks indicate a lack of understanding of the purpose of a mission statement.

These educators need to be reminded that a mission statement is a description of a preferred future, not a description of current reality. The importance of the mission statement is that, once stated, it provides us with a *clear trajectory* and the *capacity to assess* progress toward the mission. If a school mission statement only represents current reality, it will be of no value in inspiring and energizing the stakeholders, and of no use in monitoring success in achieving the mission.

Clear and Focused Mission in Action

A popular aphorism often invoked by organizational leaders is that the challenge of leadership is "to keep the main thing the main thing." Complex organizations and the people who work in them are constantly being pushed and pulled in different directions. One of the functions that falls heavily at the feet of leaders is to constantly help the workers maintain the focus on the organizational mission and core values.

Mission and Leadership

The leader's greatest contribution to the school improvement effort is to articulate a compelling vision and mission, and to convince the followers that the mission is attainable, and a moral and worthy cause. School leaders must keep the mission front and center, and see to it that every program, policy, and strategy is evaluated in light of the mission. It is especially important that the leaders work to integrate the mission into the school culture so that the mission will continue to drive teaching and learning well after the leader departs.

Practitioner Perspectives and Insights

In keeping with our efforts to track the views of practitioners about the correlates of effective schools, in the spring of 2009 we conducted a Reality Check online survey about the clear and focused mission correlate. We were primarily interested in finding out whether practitioners had a true sense of the mission, whether accountability and standards factored into their sense of the mission, and which programs, strategies, and policies they found effective in helping to focus on the mission. Two hundred twenty-seven educators responded to the survey. Forty-four percent of the respondents were associated with elementary level schools, 28 percent were from middle or high schools, and 28 percent indicated other—mostly central office.

When asked to indicate whether they perceived that the overwhelming majority of their school's staff had a true sense of mission when it came to all students mastering the essential curricular goals of the school, 79 percent agreed or strongly agreed with the statement. Approximately 15 percent disagreed or strongly disagreed with the statement.

When asked to indicate their perceptions regarding whether the accountability and standards focus has helped increase the sense of mission among stakeholder groups, 77 percent agreed or strongly agreed that it had increased the sense of mission. Only about 13 percent disagreed or strongly disagreed.

One hundred ninety respondents answered the question about programs, strategies, and policies they had found to be effective in creating a clear and focused mission. Most of the strategies, while not specific, reflected the notion of clear, frequent, and focused communication of the mission. Sometimes the communication responsibility was specifically vested with the principal and sometimes it was placed with the leadership team, professional learning community, or correlate teams. Respondents suggested that the communication should focus on making certain everyone understands the state standards and the common assessments when available.

Respondents frequently cited two specific programs or processes that were effective in focusing schools on the mission. Professional learning communities (PLCs) were suggested as an important and effective way to improve the focus on the mission. PLC at Work™, a model created by Rick DuFour, Becky DuFour, and Bob Eaker, was cited. Similarly, Doug Reeves's Data Teams were seen as a means of bringing focus to the mission of the school. We found these responses offered a favorable picture of practitioners' perceptions of the clear and focused mission correlate. We were particularly interested to see professional learning communities being identified again as a means for advancing school improvement.

Research-Supported Strategies

We have identified several studies that define strategies that are effective in implementing the clear and focused mission correlate.

Clarify core beliefs and values. For a staff to create a meaningful mission, it must define and clarify its core beliefs and values. Some examples of core beliefs that educators have used include:

- Education is a shared responsibility—Achievement requires the commitment and participation of staff, students, family, and community.

- All students can learn—All students have potential that can be developed.

- Rates of learning vary—The time required for mastery has no bearing on the value of the learner.

- All students have unique skills and talents—Individual abilities must be identified and nurtured.

- High self-esteem enhances success—People develop best through sincere praise and validation.

Core values define how individuals will act toward one another in an organization. They are the behaviors the stakeholders are committed to acting upon—that is, behaviors that would be recognized and rewarded because they illustrate the core values. Examples of core value statements include:

- All members of the school community deserve respect.

- Trust is critical to the success of the school.

- Cooperation is essential—Learning experiences must encourage and teach skills that foster cooperation.

- Optimism about people, education, and the future is key to academic success.

Cohen (1993) found that giving teachers time to talk together helped them clarify their beliefs and determine shared values. Through such discussions, teachers began to resolve inconsistencies between their goals and their behaviors in the classroom. For assistance in structuring a process for clarifying core beliefs and values, you may want to refer to the *Implementation Guide* (Lezotte & McKee, 2004), a companion manual for *Assembly Required: A Continuous School Improvement System* (Lezotte & McKee, 2002). This resource provides step-by-step activities for clarifying beliefs and values.

Involve the stakeholders. Darling-Hammond (1995) found that effective superintendents involve all stakeholders in setting goals in pursuit of the mission.

Chhuon, Gilkey, Gonzalez, Daly, and Chrispeels (2008) found that districtwide summits designed to create a common language (that is, clarify mission, beliefs, and values) significantly increased the level of trust between school staff and the central office. Allen (2001) noted that when a mission statement is developed in isolation, the staff has little personal connection to it. This approach lessens commitment (and thus, involvement) in attaining that mission.

Make the mission clear and specific. By their nature, mission statements use language that is conceptual and often abstract (for example, learning for all). While such statements serve to inspire and energize, they do not provide much guidance on what someone is expected to do next. Allen (2001) found that many mission statements are no more than plaques on the wall—the language is too vague, and the statements don't connect with results and often are too long and complicated. For example, several school districts declare their mission to be: "Prepare students for the choices and challenges they will face in the 21st century." To implement this mission, staff would need to have more details about the knowledge, skills, and dispositions students need to know and be able to do when they graduate from our schools to "be prepared for the choices and challenges they will face in the 21st century." Ideally, the process for clarifying the mission statement would be collaborative and inclusive.

Keep the focus on the mission. DuFour and Eaker (1998, p. 115) assert, "Mission, vision, values, and goals must be continually referenced in the day-to-day workings of the school. Redundancy is not only permissible—it is desirable." Allen (2001) reinforced that belief. He stated that once a mission statement is developed, there must be an ongoing dialogue that deepens people's understanding of it, and that all school programs and actions should be evaluated in light of the extent to which they further the school's mission. According to Darling-Hammond (1995), taking such steps is not easy; she found that one of the more difficult challenges for educators is to step back from good ideas if evidence indicates these ideas don't support student learning.

Developing a Data Dashboard

Virtually all schools have a formal written mission statement that exists as part of the formal archive of the school. Some statements may be short and simple, while others may be lengthy and complex. Although all schools likely have a mission statement, in only a few schools do staff seem to have a true sense of mission when it comes to implementing it and sustaining the values of the school. Obviously, the existence of a written statement is unlikely to make much difference in the behaviors of the adults in the school or the achievement of the students. Consequently, measurement strategies should focus on the extent to which there is a true and valued sense of mission among the adults.

Determining the extent to which a school demonstrates that it has a clear and focused mission requires examination of two interdependent components: (1) communication strategy and (2) broad cultural awareness. The clear and focused mission correlate is designed to zero in on the mission and core beliefs and values by which the school wishes to be defined. One of the most straightforward ways to determine whether a school has met the criteria of a clear and focused mission is to visit the school and ask staff and students at random, "What does this school care most about?" In an effective school, all the people asked will have the same answer to that question. The less-effective school is more likely to have as many different answers to that question as individuals to whom the question is addressed.

The second component requiring examination is the extent to which the sense of mission and the resulting commitment is embraced by all staff or only a select few. For example, members of the school leadership team may manifest a strong sense of mission, but staff members not on the team may not share that understanding. The goal of measuring the correlate is to assess whether a sense of mission actually exists in a school and whether the commitment is truly shared by all the adults in the school community.

Perceptual Survey Questions

The online survey tool Reality Check contains 231 survey items for the clear and focused mission correlate organized around three subareas:

1. Inclusive sense of mission
2. Translating mission into curriculum, instruction, and assessment operations
3. Alignment between intended, taught, and assessed curriculum

From this source, we have selected items that could be used to assess perceptions in these areas. Ask respondents to indicate their level of agreement (strongly agree, agree, undecided, disagree, strongly disagree, or not applicable) regarding statements such as:

- I understand the overall purpose and priorities of our school.
- There is an agreed-upon written statement of purpose that guides the instructional program.
- I am committed to the school's instructional priorities.
- Our school uses the instructional focus to provide a clear direction for the school's instructional program.
- There is little to no discussion about school goals and means of achieving them during school faculty or in-service meetings.

Self-Report Questions

Responses to open-ended questions can provide additional information in order to assess whether the staff has a sense of mission and is committed to implementing the mission. Examples of self-report questions include:

- What is the mission of this school or district?

- How do you translate the mission and priorities of the school into your everyday instructional actions in the classroom?

- How often is the mission of your school or district referenced when talking about new initiatives, policies, curriculum, and instruction?

Third-Party Direct Observations

The quality management scholar, W. Edwards Deming (1993), noted that organizations consist of two parallel systems: the *intended system* (what is actually supposed to happen) and the *actual system* (what actually does happen). In the context of the school, the intended system might be associated with the mission, formal curricular statements, standards, and curricular pacing charts. The actual system might be associated with the routine instructional experiences students have in the classroom day after day. In an organization that has a pervasive sense of mission, the actual and intended systems should match.

What happens when a student fails to learn is of particular interest in monitoring the clear and focused mission correlate. Does the teacher reteach the lesson to that student in a new or different way to facilitate understanding? Or does the teacher just move on to the next lesson, leaving struggling students behind? Whichever behavior the teacher embraces is a good indicator as to whether she is committed to the learning-for-all mission. The same holds true for the school or district as a whole. What mechanisms are in place to assist struggling students? How does the organization provide for customization and differentiation of instruction so that all students learn? The answers to these questions are strong indicators of where the head and heart of the organization lay. Remember, wherever the head and heart are, the hands are sure to follow.

Third-party direct observers could be asked to visit classrooms, record the actual student learning experiences, and compare them to what is supposed to be occurring subject by subject, grade by grade. Any discrepancy between intended and actual experiences is problematic for all students, but especially for struggling students. As they move from grade to grade not having mastered the requisite knowledge and skills, their learning deficits grow. The data obtained through third-party direct observations can be used to help teachers adjust their instructional practices, bringing them into line with the mission.

Conclusion

Despite the urgency to improve student achievement and the pressure to do something, the school community must not short-circuit the discussions around core beliefs and values and the process of developing the mission. This process ensures that everyone is pulling the wagon in the same direction.

Likewise, it's important to remember that effective schools don't just create a mission and post it on the wall. Effective schools use the mission as a guide for every policy, program, and practice that is adopted and implemented. Those schools use the mission to create a culture of learning, one that encourages students and staff and motivates them to accomplish more than they ever dreamed possible. Effective leaders use the mission to inspire the followers to action and to focus relentlessly on student learning and achievement. Effective schools not only have a clear and focused mission, they live that mission on a daily basis.

CHAPTER 6

Opportunity to Learn/Time on Task

In the effective school, teachers manage instructional time to ensure that, for a high percentage of time, students are actively engaged in teacher-directed learning activities focused on the essential skills.

The meaning of this correlate is simple: students tend to learn the things on which they spend time. The meaning seems more than obvious. But implementing the opportunity to learn/time on task correlate is far more complicated than this simple definition implies. It is not simply a matter of time.

In his book *Conditions of Learning* (1985), Robert Gagné defined learning as a relatively permanent change in one's behavior, attitude, or disposition as a result of external experiences connecting with internal states. In Gagné's definition, the confluence of these two forces must occur. The internal state of the individual learner—that composite of past learning—must connect with the individual's current experiences. When this connection is successful, learning occurs. When the connection fails, for whatever reason, the intended learning is not likely to occur. A careful consideration of this definition of learning provides insight into a profound truth and the major systems problems with which all schools struggle, but which effective schools have successfully challenged. What should schools do to ensure that students are exposed to opportunities and conditions that enable them to learn?

Opportunity to Learn and School Readiness

Learning can occur virtually anytime and anywhere. Learning can be intended or unintended, in school or out of school, alone or with others. One might say that the whole of one's life represents one gigantic opportunity to learn. Couple this with the fact that humans come into the world with a deep yearning for learning, and the ingredients exist for both human survival and human advancement.

While every human may have numerous opportunities to learn, the life experiences of individuals, while common in many ways, are also unique (Musti-Rao &

Carledge, 2007; Wasik, Bond, & Hindman, 2002). The dynamic interplay between newborns and their early life experiences creates individual differences. As children grow, these individual differences tend to increase in some areas and decrease in others. Access to books, to the spoken word, and even to healthcare can affect a child's readiness to learn (Currie, 2005). Disadvantaged students typically have less access to the important building blocks of school readiness and, as a result, enter public schools about two years (on average) behind their more advantaged counterparts (Knitzer & Lefkowitz, 2006).

The critical factor in this lifelong differentiation process that educators must recognize is that new learning tends to build on earlier learning; this is the way the brain does its vital work. These great truths matter because school learning, though intentional, occurs one student at a time. To be effective, educators must recognize that learners come from situations that provide different opportunities and bring their past learning (or lack thereof) to the classroom; it cannot be otherwise since this is who they are (Musti-Rao & Carledge, 2007).

About 65 percent of the observed gap in measured student achievement between advantaged and disadvantaged students is, first and foremost, a gap in opportunity to learn (Alexander, Entwisle, & Olson, 2007). Schools must come to accept the fact that they will never actually close the observed learning gap until they first close the opportunity-to-learn gap. Ensuring that each student is provided sufficient time and appropriate experiences to learn is the way that a school actually "walks" its mission "talk."

Opportunity to Learn and the System in Place

Many otherwise well-meaning educators often resist attending to the opportunity to learn/time on task correlate. Why? Because embracing this correlate means changing the system in place in two significant ways. First, the policy of placing all students based on their chronological age is deeply ingrained in the traditional culture of public schools. The factory model of schooling that became popular during the Industrial Revolution was based on the premise that all students have been given an equal opportunity to learn the knowledge and skills required for the individual student's current age or grade. But, as is commonly known today, disadvantaged students enter public schools about two years behind their more advantaged counterparts. Many educators want to ignore this opportunity gap since they either lack the necessary resources or are not committed to differentiating instruction. As a result, disadvantaged students who start school behind other students are often placed in a slower course of study with the hope that someday they'll catch up to the others—clearly illogical assumptions that are not supported by the research.

Second, schools resist changes that are disruptive to the established routines. The school schedule and how time is used are two longstanding traditions that define the way schools work. These traditions come from the agrarian calendar that has dominated school schedules. To eliminate some classes and increase the amount of time allocated to others represents changes in school schedules that few have been willing to undertake.

The Agrarian Calendar

The agrarian school calendar was something to be proud of as an example of a national commitment to compulsory school for all children. After all, under that calendar every child had the opportunity to attend school and be engaged in learning about six hours a day and about 180 days a year. While different states, provinces, and counties had various regulations governing the number of years students were compelled to attend (it is only fairly recently that all states in the United States require students to attend school to at least age sixteen), most provided an opportunity for students to attend publicly funded schools until they graduated from high school. In some places students were permitted to attend free public schools until they were twenty years old as long as they were demonstrating progress toward attaining a high school diploma.

The early structures and policies associated with the agrarian calendar set the deep structure and culture for today's schools, especially schools in the United States and Canada. Tyack and Cuban (1997) include these structural and cultural artifacts in what they call the "grammar" of the public school. They noted that many of the advocates of school reform want schools to improve, but they don't want educators to "mess" with the grammar of the schools. The problem with maintaining the agrarian calendar becomes evident through a study of the compelling research surrounding the correlate of opportunity to learn/time on task. This research suggests that expanding the opportunities to learn, especially for disadvantaged students, and increasing time on task for all students are among the highest-yield strategies that educators can deploy to advance student learning and performance.

The agrarian calendar is an artifact that represents an insidious challenge for today's schools struggling to meet the challenges of learning for all. To exemplify this point, let's divide the world of potential student learning into two parts: school-based learning and out-of-school learning. Even if the amount of out-of-school learning was constant, regardless of the socioeconomic background of the students, we could still make a good case for increasing time in school for all students—and an even stronger case for the disadvantaged students—as a straightforward strategy for raising achievement.

Now consider the reality: out-of-school learning differs significantly for advantaged and disadvantaged students. The research around summer learning loss (Cooper, Nye, Charlton, Lindsay, & Greathouse, 1996; Entwisle & Alexander, 1992) for disadvantaged students compared to summer gains for advantaged students makes it very difficult to imagine how the school-based learning component alone can truly close the achievement gap unless or until we are prepared to change the culture and structure of today's schools (particularly the agrarian calendar).

The Role of Technology in Expanding Time on Task and Opportunity to Learn

As computers became more relevant to K–12 education, a digital divide emerged between more affluent schools and poor schools. At first, the conversation about technology in schools focused on which schools had computers. As more schools obtained computers, the discussion focused on access to the Internet (United States Department of Education, 2003). Now that most schools have computers and access to the Internet, we are talking about the right way to use technology to promote learning. Duran (2002) found that low-income schools tended to use educational technology for remedial tasks, engaging students in academic drill and practice activities. He also found that teachers tended to match technology use with student achievement level, providing higher-achieving students with more opportunities to use technology. As a result, lower-achieving students experienced little technology usage that focused on higher-order learning. Wenglinsky (2005/2006) found that the more high school students used technology at home to complete assignments, the higher their performance on the National Assessment of Educational Progress (NAEP). Conversely, the more students used the computer in school, the more poorly they performed, likely because their computer use was limited to low-level drill and practice tasks. He emphasized that technology use for high school students must be different from that for lower grades, and should emphasize higher-order thinking skills within the context of specific content. Finally (and not insignificantly), Hug, Krajcik, and Marx (2005) found that appropriate classroom technology could increase student engagement, a critical precursor to effective learning.

Does online learning, a more recent resource for increasing time on task, hold promise for raising student learning and student performance? Unfortunately, the answer is both yes and no. If both advantaged and disadvantaged students had equal access to online technology outside of school, the proper use of that technology could contribute to the dual goals of increasing the learning and performance of all students and, at the same time, provide more time on task for the disadvantaged. In other words, educators would be leveraging one component of out-of-school learning to offset other differences between advantaged and disadvantaged students in out-of-school opportunities to learn.

Unfortunately, disadvantaged students generally lack access and opportunity to engage in online learning. This difference in access and opportunity between the SES cohorts has been described as the "digital divide." From this perspective, access to online out-of-school learning opportunities favors more advantaged students. If not addressed, this discrepancy could in fact add to the achievement gap rather than close it.

The online opportunities for high levels of student learning outside school are increasing rapidly. The momentum is building and can't be slowed, let alone stopped. This is as it should be. The fundamental challenge for school leaders is to find policies and structures that will level the playing field (both within and outside the school) to ensure that students have access and opportunity to use online technology to actually increase time on task. Online learning technologies provide resources that support students' learning "any time, any place, any path and any pace" (Florida Virtual School, 2009).

Changes in the availability of online learning were described in a report by the National American Council for Online Learning (NACOL) (Watson, Gemin, & Ryan, 2008). This study found that online learning grew throughout 2007 and the first half of 2008, in terms of both new programs and the enhancement of existing programs. During that time, many states passed new legislation to promote online learning. However, NACOL also reported that many states still had barriers to online learning, including student access to online courses, the willingness of schools to grant credit for online courses, and funding, as well as other limiting policies.

Time on Task and Essential Learnings

In any organization, large or small, there is a finite amount of resources. In education, the two most precious resources are time and human energy. The length of the school day and school year are the parameters for the resource of time. Unless one (or both) of the parameters is changed, the total available time must be thought of as a fixed and finite resource. Likewise, human energy is best thought of as a fixed resource. In this context, the single most important question that must be answered is, "How should these fixed and finite resources be allocated across the different actions and activities that constitute the typical school day?" To answer this question, we must address another: "What are the essential knowledge and skills we want our students to learn, in what order, and to what standard?

There are probably as many different ideas about what schools ought to teach and what students ought to learn as there are people who have sought to answer this question. Answering this question has become even more complicated because of the tremendous explosion of knowledge (and availability of that knowledge), as well as changing societal expectations. One of the fatal mistakes school leaders can make is to try to be all things to all people, all the time. One key to the success of the effective schools, over the years, has been the willingness of the leaders to step up and intentionally declare that some learnings matter more than others. They are willing to align both their time and human energy resources to what they have defined as the mission, core values, and beliefs.

Choosing What Matters

The context of contemporary public education can be described as a world in which there is too much to teach and not nearly enough time to teach it all well. As a result, the first obligation of a school is to reduce the world of possible learnings to a manageable program of curriculum and instruction. The accountability and standards movement has led to a serious problem of curriculum overload. In many states and provinces, mandated standards are overly ambitious, especially for schools seeking to ensure mastery for economically poor and disadvantaged students.

Despite the good intentions of advocates of the standards and accountability movement, many school reform efforts have failed. A primary reason for those failures is that, in every case, schools were asked to do more! Leaders of effective schools address the problem of being asked to do more head on. They are willing to declare that some things are more important than others, and to abandon some less-important content so that the students have time to master the critical content in the limited time available. Effective educational leaders help the teachers become more skilled at implementing interdisciplinary curriculum and at practicing what Lawrence Lezotte calls "organized abandonment." They learn to ask, answer, and deliver on the question, "What goes and what stays?"

To drive the point home, let's compare the teacher to a carpenter. When the carpenter goes to a job site, he expects to find two things: (1) a clear blueprint of the house to be built and (2) sufficient raw materials to do the job. Similarly, when arriving at the classroom, a teacher has the right to expect a curricular blueprint and the necessary raw materials (for example, time). If the job to be done is too big for the time available, one of two adjustments must be made. Either the size of the job must be scaled back (for example, drop Shakespeare and keep grammar), or we can go as far as we can until we run out of time (for example, teach a little Shakespeare and a little grammar, neither very well). The latter approach is far too common among schools in the United States. Roth and Garnier (2006/2007) found that the word that best describes science teaching in the American schools was *variety*, indicating a lack of specific, coherent science content. In another study, McTighe, Seif, and Wiggins (2004) reported that Japanese teachers cover far less ground in mathematics than their American counterparts, but emphasize a deeper understanding of math concepts.

Who should be held accountable when the resources don't match the task at hand? Certainly not the carpenter! The architect who designed the blueprints and ordered the materials is responsible for such a mismatch. Clearly then, the school leadership is responsible for seeing that the scope and depth of what the school is required to teach matches the time and resources available.

Curriculum Alignment and Opportunity to Learn

Curriculum alignment is an opportunity-to-learn issue, one that carries with it a moral imperative. If the intended, taught, and tested curricula are not aligned, students pay the price. No matter how hard they work, students will never meet the specified standards if those standards aren't taught in the schools. How can the adults in the school justify this situation—in effect, penalizing the students most in need, those who depend almost completely on the school for content learning—simply because alignment issues have not been addressed? Lack of alignment affects more than just students; school leaders and teachers are also affected. In a world where schools are held accountable for student learning and performance, any perceived disconnect between the intended, the taught, and the assessed curricula causes high levels of anxiety for students and staff when student assessments are administered. When anxiety levels reach untenable levels, staff may begin to behave in improper and desperate ways.

Opportunity to Learn/Time on Task in Action

As educators move to implement the opportunity to learn/time on task correlate, they must be sensitive to the factors that apply to each concept. Opportunity to learn involves recognizing students' individual differences and their readiness for new learning, accommodating those differences through adjustments in the curriculum and delivery of instruction, and aligning the intended, taught, and assessed curricula. Time on task has both institutional and individual implications. Institutionally, this correlate requires educators to determine how the school calendar is organized, on a yearly and a daily basis. Changing the yearly calendar is outside the jurisdiction of individual schools and districts. However, school leaders can determine how best to schedule time during the school day to provide the best possible use of available resources to benefit student learning. The concepts of opportunity to learn and time on task are inextricably linked through the specifics of essential learnings. Leaders of effective schools make sound choices about what best serves students in achieving success and what best serves teachers in carrying out their professional responsibilities. The principle of equity in quality incorporates all of these factors.

Practitioner Perspectives and Insights

In the spring of 2009, we conducted an online Reality Check survey that addressed opportunity to learn/time on task. Of the 227 educators who responded, 44 percent were associated with elementary level schools, 28 percent were from middle or high schools, and 28 percent indicated other—mostly central office. The survey included statements about the effect of opportunity to learn on the achievement gap, the extent to which students are engaged in essential learning activities, and use of time within the school. It also included statements about the effect of the standards, accountability, and assessment movement, as well as programs, policies, or practices that supported the correlate. Respondents were asked to indicate their level of agreement with each of the statements.

Respondents were asked to indicate the extent to which they agreed with the idea that the achievement gap between advantaged and disadvantaged students will not be able to be closed until the opportunity-to-learn gap is closed first. Eighty percent agreed or strongly agreed with the statement, while 10 percent were undecided, and 11 percent disagreed or strongly disagreed. This degree of agreement with the idea of closing the opportunity gap strongly suggests that schools should be very focused on understanding and eliminating gaps in opportunity structures and experiences for disadvantaged students.

Forty-one percent of respondents believed that students are actively engaged in essential learning activities about 60 to 80 percent of the time. An additional 35 percent indicated that they thought students were actively engaged in essential learning activities more than 80 percent of the time. The perceptions of the student engagement rate, as seen by these respondents, seems to be much higher than has been reported by research studies over the years.

When asked to indicate their degree of agreement with the statement, "The goal of learning for all cannot be realized without increasing the amount of time available for teaching and learning," 70 percent agreed or strongly agreed, while 22 percent disagreed or strongly disagreed.

When asked to indicate their agreement or disagreement with the statement that the accountability and assessment movement has "narrowed the curriculum to a dangerous level and important student learnings are being pushed aside," 65 percent agreed or strongly agreed, and only 24 percent disagreed or strongly disagreed.

When asked to indicate whether the number of standards students are expected to master in a given grade or content area are realistic or unrealistic, 65 percent indicated the number was unrealistic or very unrealistic; only 23 percent believed the number was realistic or very realistic.

A total of 216 individuals responded to this open-ended question: would it be better to have fewer standards and focus more on the *quality* of instruction rather than the *quantity* of the content to be learned? By a factor of five to one, the respondents expressed the view that education generally and the learners specifically would be better served with fewer standards. Many suggested that we should place less emphasis on passing the test and more emphasis on mastery of the power standards and essential learnings. Some felt that the focus would be fine if we were to eliminate nonessential learnings.

Another part of the survey asked respondents about programs or strategies they had found to be effective in addressing the gaps in the opportunity to learn for various groups in their schools. The 190 individuals who responded offered a wide array of responses. Using existing time wisely and focusing on good instruction were the two responses most frequently cited. Several respondents suggested using grant monies to extend the day for those students who need more help and to provide tutoring and mentoring options. Additional suggestions included differentiating instruction, providing more hands-on experiences, consistently monitoring student progress, and utilizing data-based diagnostic procedures and formative assessments.

The respondents were also asked to describe what strategies they were using in their schools to increase learning time for struggling students. The most frequently cited strategies focused on adding to the length of the school day, either before or after school, for tutoring or small-group instruction. In an extension of the same idea, many respondents spoke about various summer programs. A few noted that they were using intersession periods to help struggling students catch up and keep up.

In addition to actually adding time to the school day or year, several respondents indicated that they had used strategies that redeployed the current school time to meet a different set of priorities. For example, some schools were using double periods to give extra time for reading. Other schools decided to eliminate one elective and use that time for extra instruction in a needed area. The responses of practitioners who completed our survey of the opportunity to learn/time on task correlate were generally consistent with findings from selected research studies that we examine in the next section.

Research-Supported Strategies

Identify the power standards. Noted author Douglas Reeves (2000), in an article titled "Standards Are Not Enough: Essential Transformations for School Success," suggested that educational leaders seeking to pare down the curriculum identify the power standards—those that meet three criteria:

1. Endurance—Does the standard provide students with knowledge and skills that will be of value beyond a single test?

2. Leverage—Will the standard provide knowledge and skills that are applicable across a wide spectrum of other disciplines?

3. Readiness—Will the standard provide students with the knowledge and skills necessary to be successful at the next level of learning?

Align the curriculum. Teachers must be engaged in the process from the beginning (Turner, 2003). To ensure their participation and commitment, administrators must allot adequate time for the alignment process; ensure that the process remains focused and relevant to teachers; involve teachers in developing instructional pacing charts; review content standards across disciplines and grades; and encourage teachers to share ideas, tips, and effective instructional practices.

Offer a rich learning environment to all students. One study comparing low-socioeconomic status (SES) classrooms to high-SES classrooms found that there are substantial and widespread differences in student access to the print experiences and environments that are considered critical to literacy development and achievement. Students in low-SES classrooms had smaller libraries, less exposure to extended text materials, and less choice over what they read and wrote—in other words, less opportunity to learn (Duke, 2000).

Foster effective classroom management among staff. Disruptive, unruly students disturb the class and steal time from instruction. Marzano and Marzano (2003) found that, of all the variables studied, classroom management had the largest effect on student achievement. They asserted that effective classroom management keeps students on task, engages their interest in the subject matter, and maintains a safe and orderly environment, all conditions that have been found to promote high student achievement. Rather than leaving the establishment of teacher-student relationships to chance, teachers need to adopt strategies that research has shown will build these relationships and, in turn, support high student achievement.

Think outside the box. Wahlstrom (2002) reported on a school district that changed the high school start time from 7:15 a.m. to 8:40 a.m. This time change had a significant effect on several variables that influence student learning and behavior; changes were observed in the areas of increased attendance, reduced tardiness, depression, and daytime sleepiness, as well as better attitudes toward homework and test preparation.

Address the opportunity-to-learn gap before children start kindergarten. Two significant studies found that students who participated in the Chicago Child-Parent Center Preschool Programs were much less likely to be put in special education and had lower dropout rates (Conyers, Reynolds, & Ou, 2003; Ou & Reynolds, 2006).

Address the summer learning gap. Alexander et al. (2007) offered one of the clearest pictures of how poverty and schooling interact to create the generational effects of poverty. The study also reported on the long-term impact of the summer learning gap. In this study, the initial test score gap in first grade between these two groups (low-SES and high-SES students) was found to be 26.48 points. At the end of the nine-year study, the gap between the two groups had increased to 73.16 points. The researchers' most significant conclusions centered on what they called the "seasonality of learning." They noted that the lack of improvement in cognitive achievement during the summer season for the low-SES students represents the bridge between summer learning shortfall over the elementary school years and the outcomes in later schooling. Borman and Dowling (2006) found that summer school programs increased student achievement, but only when students participated regularly.

Improve the quality of teaching. Simply put, high-quality teachers are synonymous with opportunity to learn. Kati Haycock (1998), in a review of several studies, found that high-quality teaching was crucial to improving student achievement. She cited one study in Dallas, Texas, in which the average reading scores of fourth graders assigned to three highly effective teachers in a row rose from the 59th percentile in fourth grade to the 76th percentile by the end of sixth grade. In contrast, students who were taught by ineffective teachers experienced a drop of 15 percentile points over the same period. She identified two factors that are characteristic of high-quality teachers: strong verbal and math skills, and deep content knowledge.

Add quality, not just time. A report by Education Research Services (Molineaux, 2008) reviewed four alternative scheduling practices: block scheduling, year-round school, school start times, and adding time to the schedule. Issues analyst Rebecca Molineaux looked at the pros and cons of each, and found one common element among the practices: simply increasing seat time for students, whatever the format adopted, is not enough to improve student achievement. The time added must be high-quality instructional time. The same finding applies to summer school. In a review of summer school programs, Denton (2002) found that those that were successful didn't just offer more of the same—the programs that were effective in raising student achievement had high-quality teachers, a climate of innovation and creativity, and a comprehensive evaluation plan.

Engage students. According to Phillip C. Schlechty, author of *Working on the Work* (2002), engagement precedes learning. In a study on mathematics learning in elementary school, Bodovski and Farkas (2007) found that student engagement had a positive effect at all grade levels tested (K–3). The students in the lowest group had the most benefit from being engaged with the subject matter. Conversely, the students in the lowest group showed the least gains when they were disengaged. Interestingly, student engagement was found to have more of an impact on achievement scores than the amount of instruction.

Differentiate instruction. Opportunity to learn means that instruction is tailored to student needs. Caroline McCullen (2003) suggested that technology can facilitate differentiation because it can offer more time on task without the teacher, as well as present content in different ways to meet the needs of students' different learning styles. However, McCullen cautioned that technology should not be limited to simple drill-and-practice programs, which in some cases may do more harm than good. Rather, more effective uses of technology should include "simulations and complex processes that activate higher levels of thinking" (p. 36). Tomlinson (1999, p. 11) suggested that although there is no single formula for creating a differentiated classroom, some key ideas should be kept in mind. The teacher has to be clear about the essential principles, concepts, and skills students are expected to master, and use daily assessments to adjust instruction. Tomlinson emphasized that "you need not differentiate all elements in all possible ways. Effective differentiated classrooms include many times in which whole-class, nondifferentiated fare is the order of the day" (p. 11).

Developing a Data Dashboard

Seemingly one of the best-kept secrets in American education is that students do, in fact, tend to learn those things they are actually taught. If educators doubt the truthfulness of this statement, they should examine the relationship between how much time children spend watching their favorite television program and how well they learn the content of that program.

This being so, it becomes clear that two conditions must be met for intended learning to occur. First, learners must have access and opportunity to learn the intended curriculum, and second, once given access and opportunity, they must put forth the time and effort needed to learn. These conditions are sequential— access and opportunity must precede the investment of time and effort. Closing the opportunity-to-learn gap is the critical first step educators must take if they hope to close the actual learning gaps between advantaged and disadvantaged students.

Continuous school improvement requires that schools develop appropriate tools to assess and monitor the opportunity structures available to all students and the time and effort the learners devote to the instructional task. Consider the situation in which a student performs poorly on an achievement test the teacher administers. Given the student's results, the teacher needs to identify the source of the poor performance. What data, in addition to the test score, should the teacher examine? Initially, the teacher should look for evidence that the student had legitimate access and opportunity to learn the intended curriculum. Next, the teacher should check evidence that documents the student's investment of time and effort.

The opportunity to learn/time on task correlate is one of the most directly observable, measurable correlates. Time on task can be calculated at many different levels, including, for example, the length of the actual school year at either state, province, or district levels. Even this relatively crude measure reveals rather large differences in intended time on task across these jurisdictions. Examining the school schedule provides data on how many minutes per day, week, or year students are intended to be on task in each class or content area. These data will reveal substantial variance in the intended time on the various learning tasks across schools and districts.

Opportunity to Learn

Opportunity to learn is a seemingly simple concept that may prompt educators who are convinced they provided adequate opportunity to conclude that a student who fails to learn didn't invest the necessary time and effort. Before coming to this conclusion, educators must consider another less obvious aspect of opportunity to learn: the student's level of prior learning. Robert Marzano (2004) found that the correlation between prerequisite knowledge and new learning was found to be around $r = 0.70$. The strength of this relationship suggests that if a student lacks critical prior knowledge upon which the new learning builds, that student is being denied a legitimate opportunity to learn the new content. The extent to which teachers ensure that all students have opportunity to learn can be examined through perceptual surveys, self reports, and third-party direct observations.

Perceptual Survey Questions

The effective schools online survey included about 135 items designed to survey a respondent's perceptions pertaining to the correlate of opportunity to learn/time on task. Using such statements as those that follow, educators can obtain data that reveal the presence or absence, strength or weakness of opportunity to learn in the school and individual classrooms. Ask respondents to indicate their level of agreement (strongly agree, agree, undecided, disagree, strongly disagree, or not applicable) regarding statements such as:

- As a teacher, I am encouraged to modify the curriculum to meet the students' needs.

- Allocated instructional time can be flexible to meet the curricular, instructional, and assessment needs of teachers and students.

- Enhanced instruction is routinely provided for low-achieving students.

Self-Report Questions

Responses to open-ended questions can provide additional insights into what individual teachers experience as they strive to ensure that their programs and practices engage all the students. These questions are examples from our Reality Check online survey of opportunity to learn:

- What percent of the students in your class were performing at or above grade-level standards at the beginning of the current school year?

- How do you routinely assess student readiness before planning and delivering classroom lessons?

- How do you best compensate for the fact that poor and disadvantaged students often lack critical background knowledge, especially when it comes to language development?

Third-Party Direct Observations

The range of information that could be gathered and examined by third-party observation is virtually limitless. The observer should carefully examine lesson plans to determine how the assessments of student readiness are built into the plans. Data from the lesson plans should show the accommodations that the teacher intends to make to draw upon and extend students' use of prior knowledge relevant to the lesson. During observation sessions, the observer can determine the extent and appropriateness of the adjustments the teacher makes to the observed individual differences within the classroom.

Time on Task

Once appropriate accommodations have been made to provide each student a legitimate opportunity to learn the intended curriculum, the focus shifts to the amount of time allocated for the learning and the extent to which each student is appropriately engaged in the planned instructional tasks. Items from our online survey of the correlate opportunity to learn/time on task are shown to illustrate the extent to which teachers take time on task into consideration during instruction.

Perceptual Survey Questions

Teachers' responses to these statements will reveal the extent of variation in their perspectives on how time is allocated and actually used, as well as the nature of staff involvement in reaching decisions about the use of time. Ask respondents to indicate their level of agreement (strongly agree, agree, undecided, disagree, strongly disagree, or not applicable) regarding statements such as:

- Sufficient time is allocated to teach the intended learning outcomes written in the planned content areas.

- In our school, the staff determines the appropriate time allocations necessary to achieve the learning objectives.

- In order to ensure that all students master the intended content, the instructional process provides more time for students who need it.

- Teachers routinely use strategies such as reteaching and regrouping to ensure student mastery of assigned tasks.

Self-Report Questions

Teachers' responses to open-ended questions may be even more revealing about time on task factors. Recall that respondents to our online survey of high expectations for success indicated that time was a factor affecting their ability to fulfill their expectation that all students can learn to a proficient level. The responses to these open-ended questions can reveal how teachers handle the familiar complaint of "so much to do, so little time":

- Do you believe you have enough instructional time in the school day to successful teach the essential curriculum to a level of student mastery?

- What did you do in the past week to provide more time for struggling students without ignoring the students who are prepared to move forward in the curriculum?

- For each student in your class, please rate the level of engagement: generally engaged, engaged some, but not generally most of the time, disengaged most of the time.

Tally sheets can be useful for collecting self-report data. To find out the extent to which interruptions affect instructional time, teachers could tally the number, type, and length of interruptions during a selected class over the period of one week. Such reporting can provide valuable insights into the amount of time that is actually being used for instruction. Similarly, these data can be used to determine the reasons for the interruptions and to establish actions that can be taken to deal with them. Note, too, that this approach to examining time on task is useful with third-party direct observations.

Third-Party Direct Observations

The stated curriculum and the pacing charts that teachers develop as guides to the delivery of instruction are vital. From these sources, an observer can obtain a general view of projections for time allocations. However, direct observations will reveal the most important piece of information about time on task: how much of the available time for teaching and learning is actually devoted to instruction. An observer would report on the number and length of disruptions, in specified units of time, across the instructional day. Observing the engagement of students (randomly selected from a subset) in the class provides additional information about time on task. Such observations taken in several or all the classes can provide a useful picture of the rate of student engagement across the school. In this strategy, student engagement is defined as the student actually doing what the teacher has asked her to do at the moment of the observation (Lezotte & McKee, 2004).

Well-organized lessons are considered to be one of the best preventative strategies that teachers can use to manage classroom discipline effectively. With this in mind, the third-party observer could focus specifically on those students who routinely disrupt the class. The aim of such observations would be to identify what might be the cause of the problem for these students, and more importantly, what might help the teacher reduce the disruptions and increase the engagement of these students.

Conclusion

The correlate of opportunity to learn/time on task is the tangible expression of two other correlates, high expectations for success and clear and focused mission. If all the members of the school staff expect all children to learn, and concentrate their minds, hearts, and hands on the mission of making it happen, then they will see to it that every child has an equal opportunity to learn and sufficient time on task to succeed.

We know that a significant portion of the gap in achievement between advantaged and disadvantaged students is due first to a gap in opportunity to learn. How much of this differential in opportunity to learn derives from a gap in resources (for example, effective teachers, quality instructional materials, or money) cannot be precisely stated. We do know, however, that a substantial gap in opportunity to learn occurs when disadvantaged students are taught by less-experienced teachers, in less well-equipped and older schools, with dated curricular materials. And we also know that we can never hope to close the actual learning gap until we first close the opportunity-to-learn gap.

CHAPTER 7

Frequent Monitoring of Student Progress

In an effective school, student progress is monitored frequently using a variety of assessment procedures. Assessment results are used to improve individual student performance and to adapt the instructional program to meet student learning needs.

The clear and focused mission correlate represents the intent of school relative to student learning and student performance. The opportunity to learn/time on task correlate represents the actions the learners actually experience. The frequent monitoring of student progress correlate represents the impact of what teachers are doing on the intermittent and final scores for individual students, subgroups of students, and the class as a whole.

Monitoring student progress can be viewed in two different ways. First, the results can be viewed as summative in nature. In this sense, student performance on the assessment is like the final score of a football game. In most instances, today's accountability and assessment systems treat the student scores as final in that they are part of the official record, published in the newspaper, and used to mete out sanctions.

Second, and more importantly, given the learning-for-all mission, monitoring student progress can be viewed as formative. In this context, the student progress information is viewed more like the results of a practice session or scrimmage. In the scrimmage, the coach uses the performance results to make adjustments, acknowledge strengths, and work on weaknesses. The results of formative assessments represent an invaluable source of feedback that teachers can use to help individual students, small groups of students, and the class as a whole.

The primary emphasis in the effective school is to use assessment information as the basis for changing the instructional game plan. The data coming from the study of effective schools indicate that the more frequently student progress is monitored and instruction is adjusted accordingly, the more quickly the school will achieve its learning-for-all mission.

Frequent Monitoring—More Than Testing

Over the years, critics of effective schools research and practices have complained that schools have placed too much emphasis on test scores. But the fact is, schools do not have to get bogged down in paper-and-pencil tests unless they choose to do so. Testing is but one part of the monitoring process. Effective monitoring—that is, monitoring that actually leads to improved student achievement—must be defined as any review of student work that is accompanied by timely corrective feedback. Monitoring may be based on a variety of activities including oral responses, written assignments, teacher-student conferences, teacher-made tests, and observations of student performance.

Given our definition of effective monitoring, many formal tests students are required to take—such as standardized norm-referenced tests or state-mandated standards-based tests—don't qualify because of the huge lag between the tests' administration and the provision of results to the teacher and the student. To qualify as effective monitoring, a test must be followed with corrective feedback almost immediately so the teacher can adjust instruction and the student can improve. In many cases, students may not receive the test results for months, and sometimes into the next school year. When they do receive the results, they only see an aggregate score, not feedback on particular questions or problems. Clearly then, in the pursuit of improving student performance, we can see that these tests are of little or no help.

School leaders seeking to develop a management system for this correlate would be well served to insist on a variety of sources (for example, projects, oral reports, written assignments, or portfolios) to monitor student progress. Classroom assessments that provide ongoing evidence of student mastery of classroom instruction provide a more complete picture of what students' performance actually looks like and will be far more motivating to the students (Stiggins, 2004).

The Critical Role of Feedback

Credible and timely feedback from a trusted individual is one of the most powerful influences on human learning. The power of appropriate feedback ranks in the top five of over one hundred variables known to influence human learning (Hattie & Timperley, 2007). This fact alone should place appropriate uses of feedback as one of the central topics of preservice teacher preparation and ongoing teacher development. Further in their research, Hattie and Timperley reported that feedback is not effectively used in the majority of classrooms. This finding gives additional support to our position that teachers must learn appropriate uses of feedback.

The following hypothetical experiment will illustrate why feedback is so critical. Suppose a group of thirty students are randomly assigned to one of three groups. Each group of ten students is asked to play a computer game in which the goal is to keep a racecar on the track for the duration of the game. Each student's final score is based on the number of times the car goes off the track during the exercise. Low scores are preferred. All groups are encouraged to do their best, but each group is given a different treatment in our experiment.

For the first group, the screen is blocked so students cannot see how they are doing during the race. When they receive their final score, which is likely pretty dismal, they are encouraged to try harder and do better on their next attempt. The second group can see the computer screen as the task is completed, but the view on the screen shows the student where the racecar was four seconds earlier—in other words, there is a delay or lag in the feedback. Finally, the third group can see the racecar on the screen in real time. Under these treatment conditions, which group of students do you think will perform the best? The students who receive real-time feedback, of course! Real-time feedback allows the students to constantly monitor and adjust their performances. The same is true with classroom learning and performance.

Tutoring is effective because it allows the tutor to provide real-time feedback to the student. Likewise, world-class or exceptional performances by athletes and musicians are almost always associated with the performer having a personal coach. Immediate feedback from a credible tutor, coach, or mentor is another principle of human learning that can make a big difference in learning. Monitoring a learner's progress followed by feedback in near real time is an effective strategy regardless of the age of the learner, or subject matter being learned. The frequent monitoring of student progress correlate focuses directly on the importance of feedback that is timely and appropriate.

How Frequent Is Frequent?

Teachers and school leaders are always quick to ask, "How frequently should student progress be monitored?" The question is best answered with another question: how frequently can the teacher adjust instruction? If the teacher or school is prepared to adjust instruction every ten minutes, student progress should be monitored every ten minutes. If the teacher can only adjust instruction once a week, the teacher should monitor student progress once a week. On the other hand, if the teacher or the school is not going to adjust what they are planning to do based on the results of student monitoring, why bother monitoring at all? The only purpose for monitoring without adjusting instruction is to sort and select students.

The Just-in-Time Intervention System

Monitoring student performance and providing feedback are inseparable actions. The more frequent the monitoring, the more precise and timely the feedback. The faster the feedback is delivered, the more monitoring contributes to improved learning by helping build a just-in-time information and intervention system. In a just-in-time intervention system, help comes immediately and in sufficient quantity and quality to effectively and efficiently assist the learner in meeting the instructional objective. This system requires the frequent monitoring of key work processes, followed by corrective feedback and knowledge-based adjustments in those processes. This system is designed to provide the teacher with the information she needs to make changes in instruction as quickly as possible. Some instructional adjustments will be made for a single learner, some for small groups, and still others for the entire class. Of course the development and implementation of such a system will require adequate and ongoing professional development, reflective and collaborative learning and practice, and the expectation that all students can learn.

The Consequences of Inadequate Monitoring

What happens when this correlate is not in place? Without a doubt, students pay the price. Lacking frequent assessment and timely feedback, students may struggle without intervention for months, falling further and further behind their peers. Such students slowly disengage from school and eventually give up, hopeless that they will ever catch up (Barton, 2005). Their chances of being retained rise exponentially, as does their potential for dropping out of school. The costs of dropping out are dramatic, for both the student and society.

Likewise, the lack of frequent monitoring in a school negatively affects the staff. High-stakes testing for accountability is here to stay, along with the threat of punitive action for schools that perform poorly. When performance data are used only for accountability, separate from a positive culture of continuous improvement, stress increases for both staff and students, and student scores show less positive results. The best teachers tend to transfer out of schools labeled as failing, leaving students with less-qualified teachers (Darling-Hammond & Rustique-Forrester, 2005). It's no surprise that Kerr, Marsh, Iketomo, Darilek, and Barney (2006) found that teachers in high-performing schools found data empowering, while teachers in poverty-ridden, low-performing schools felt devalued and disenfranchised.

When the frequent monitoring of student progress correlate is in place, schools embrace what we call two critical principles of effective schools: the prevention principle and the responsive principle. Clearly, the most cost-effective and efficient way to solve academic problems is to prevent them in the first place. That is the prevention principle. A companion to this principle is the responsive principle. The core of this principle is that as soon as a student begins to struggle academically in any subject, help comes immediately and in sufficient quantity and quality to effectively and efficiently assist the learner in meeting the instructional objective. Both principles require a system that provides data on students' prior knowledge as well as gains in student learning (Marzano, 2003). The responsive principle is synonymous with the just-in-time intervention system.

Frequent Monitoring and High-Stakes Testing

We would be remiss if we didn't discuss the frequent monitoring of student progress correlate and its relationship to high-stakes testing. After all, all fifty states now have tests to evaluate student progress. The requirements of No Child Left Behind reinforced testing as the primary way to measure student progress and hold schools accountable for student performance. Yet on the Program in International Student Assessment (PISA) tests in 2006, the United States was 35th among the forty participating countries in mathematics, and 31st in science. That represents a decline from three years earlier. Linda Darling-Hammond and Laura McCloskey (2008) suggest that the U.S. approach to testing may significantly contribute to the bleak performance of American students.

Darling-Hammond and McCloskey found that there is a significant difference in testing approaches between the United States and the countries that outperformed it on PISA. In the United States, tests primarily use multiple-choice items that evaluate recall and recognition of discrete facts. This approach is in sharp contrast to the other countries that emphasize project-based, inquiry-oriented learning, followed by student development of products and reports or presentations to demonstrate what they have learned. These approaches are part of the examination scoring system and lead to an emphasis on development of higher-order thinking skills and the use of knowledge to solve problems. Such assessments evaluate what students can do rather than just evaluating what they know.

The approach to testing in these nations shows a greater blending of state, province, and local assessments than occurs in the United States. The local tests frequently complement centralized tests and account for up to 50 percent of a student's final examination score. The local tests are correlated to the standards or syllabus and represent critical skills, topics, and concepts in the curriculum. They are usually designed, administered, and scored locally. Teachers are allowed considerable discretion to administer the tasks as appropriate at the classroom level. In contrast to traditional, standardized tests, this approach permits teachers to obtain information and provide feedback when needed, which fosters improvement in the quality of teaching and learning. The tasks that will be required of students on the tests are not kept secret; rather, teachers know what skills their students need to develop and how students will be expected to demonstrate them.

This approach is quite different from that of devising tests and setting cut scores. These high-achieving countries have integrated centralized testing with an in-depth process of frequent monitoring with immediate feedback.

Frequent Monitoring in Action

Fair or not, members of an organization often infer the values and priorities of the organization by how its school personnel spend their time and focus their attention. When school and classroom leaders routinely monitor student achievement, provide students with timely and appropriate feedback, and make appropriate adjustments, it is easy to see that student success is the main mission. Making frequent monitoring an organizational priority is one of the best strategies leaders have at their disposal. The following section offers more specifics as to how to operationalize this correlate.

Frequent Monitoring and Leadership

Frequent monitoring means using data to guide instructional decisions. Effective use of data depends on how well the leaders in the school—principal, assistant principal, teacher leaders, and department chairs—guide the process (Kerr et al., 2006; Lachat & Smith, 2005). While the culture of education has not historically embraced the ongoing collection and analysis of data, we have evidence (from our spring 2009 Reality Check online survey for the frequent monitoring of student progress correlate) that this situation is changing. It is up to the leaders to initiate and nurture a school culture that embraces data as the way to improve school learning. To create such a culture, school leaders need to take two important steps:

1. Develop an effective data management system that is timely, comprehensive, and coherent, and has a level of continuity that provides information on student progress over time.

2. Ensure that staff members receive the training they need to utilize data effectively and efficiently in instructional decision-making.

Educational leaders must also ensure that teachers have the flexibility to address instructional needs that are uncovered by classroom assessments (Kerr et al., 2006).

Practitioner Perspectives and Insights

In the spring of 2009, 227 educators responded to an online Reality Check survey about the frequent monitoring of student progress correlate. Forty-four percent of the respondents were associated with elementary level schools, 28 percent were from middle or high schools and 28 percent indicated other—mostly central office. The survey included questions about the effect of the standards and accountability movement on the amount of testing done in the school, educators' knowledge of feedback, the existence of formative assessment practices in the school, and policies, programs, or procedures useful for monitoring student progress and instructional programs.

When asked whether the accountability and standards movement has forced schools to do too much testing, 50 percent of the respondents agreed or strongly agreed. On the other hand, 36 percent indicated that they disagreed or strongly disagreed. The remainder—about 15 percent—were uncertain about the amount of testing being required.

Respondents were nearly evenly divided in their agreement and disagreement with this statement: "Most educators are knowledgeable about the power of feedback and the best models for providing useful feedback to their learners." Forty-eight percent indicated that they agreed or strongly agreed, 41 percent disagreed or strongly disagreed, and 12 percent were uncertain.

The statement about the existence and use of a formative assessment in their schools produced one of the most overwhelmingly one-sided responses from the practitioners. Eighty-seven percent responded in the affirmative. Sixty-eight percent also answered in the affirmative when asked whether they thought that classroom teachers found formative assessments useful in advancing student learning. Twenty-one percent were unsure, and only 10 percent answered in the negative.

We received responses from 171 individuals to this question: what policies, programs or procedures have you found to be most useful in monitoring student progress and instructional programs? The responses were varied. Some respondents specified such assessments as *Measures of Academic Progress, Dynamic Indicators of Basic Early Literacy Skills (DIBELS)*, or running records as helpful monitoring strategies. These three early literacy tools are widely used by school psychologists, literacy specialists, and most early elementary teachers. However, most of the responses were more general and varied on the theme of having administrators monitor student performance data on a regular basis (for example, every grading period) or as part of the principal walkthrough strategy. Many other responses placed the monitoring responsibility with teacher teams of one sort or another (for example, PLCs, grade-level groups, or correlate teams). Finally, there was wide variation in how frequently the monitoring process (whatever form) was deployed. Frequency ranged from monitoring strategies that occurred every two or three weeks to those that occurred only once a semester or maybe three times throughout the school year. We would question whether those schools that monitor student performance only a few times a year have clear understanding of, or commitment to, this correlate.

Research-Based Strategies

We have identified several research-based strategies that provide criteria that are helpful in implementing the frequent monitoring of student progress correlate.

Institutionalize feedback. Hattie and Timperley (2007) assert that the main purpose of feedback is to reduce the discrepancies between a student's current understanding and performance and an instructional goal. They suggest a "feedback framework" that incorporates feedback about the product the student produces and the process the student used, engages the student in self-evaluation, and motivates the student to move forward.

Adjust instruction. James Popham (2008) offers a four-step framework for teachers to make instructional adjustments: identify assessment occasions, select assessment procedures, establish adjustment triggers, and make instructional adjustments.

Reach beyond standardized tests with authentic assessment. Authentic assessment helps students learn how to judge and refine their own work and efforts before, during, and after completing a project. This process requires student reflection through such activities as keeping logs about their academic work, with notes and thoughts about the decisions they made as learners; engaging in lively discussions; and participating in interview sessions with peers to discuss particular projects and the processes they used (Perone, 1991).

Use formative assessment to foster teacher collaboration. Fisher, Grant, Frey, and Johnson (2007/2008) found that a formative assessment approach became a vehicle to increase collaboration to guide and improve instruction. The pursuit of detailed knowledge about student understanding produced a model that included four steps: (1) develop pacing guides; (2) design common assessments; (3) conduct item analysis; and (4) engage in instructional conversation. They used a commercial software program to analyze test items. The results of this analysis helped staff identify trends, interventions, and other opportunities for improvement. Lachat and Smith (2005) clearly demonstrated how teacher collaboration in analyzing and interpreting the data is key to creating ownership and motivation. As the teams received accurate and timely data, the researchers noted that they began to "own" the data, use the data to solve their problems, and believe in the power of the data.

Developing a Data Dashboard

The central tenet of the continuous improvement process is "monitor and adjust, monitor and adjust!" The frequent monitoring of student progress correlate represents the educational equivalent of this tenet as found in effective schools. Since the beginning of schools and schooling, teachers have created their own tests to monitor student learning. In this respect, they have always engaged in at least half the process—monitoring. Thus, the concept of frequent monitoring shouldn't be new or strange for the typical teacher. However, the second part of the expression—"and adjust"—seems strange to a lot of well-intentioned educators. As discussed previously in this chapter, the primary aim of this correlate is to monitor individual and group performance in order to make adjustments in what follows. If a teacher delivers a lesson, assesses performance at the end of the lesson, and despite some students not reaching mastery goes on to the next lesson, that teacher is not being true to the principle of frequent monitoring of student progress. Finding out why this happens is important to ensuring that this correlate is implemented effectively.

The standards and accountability movement has provided most schools with annual assessments in at least a few content areas. Unfortunately, these high-stakes assessment programs are limited as measures of the monitoring correlate for two reasons. First, these assessments are typically only given once a year and, for some content areas, even less frequently. Meaningful assessment data needs to be collected much more frequently if it is going to provide a useful basis for adjusting instruction. Second, the elapsed time between when the high-stakes assessments are administered and results are available means that teachers cannot use the data to make timely adjustments in instruction. Meaningful use of assessment results is possible only when the time span between testing and when results are available is short (not months, as is often the case with high-stakes assessment programs). Whether or not high-stakes assessments are useful to student learning, we are sure that these programs are going to be part of school life for as far into the future as we can see. But if schools are going to capitalize on the power of the monitoring correlate, they need to develop their own supplemental monitoring system; many schools and districts have already done so.

With these factors in mind, here are some suggestions for the data dashboard for assessing the frequent monitoring of student progress.

Perceptual Survey Questions

The Reality Check survey includes 197 items designed to survey a respondent's perceptions pertaining to the correlate of frequent monitoring of student progress. Following are some examples of items that can be used to determine the presence or absence, strength or weakness of this correlate in a school and its classrooms. Ask respondents to indicate their level of agreement (strongly agree, agree, undecided, disagree, strongly disagree, or not applicable) regarding statements such as:

- Approximately every two months there is some formalized skill testing in basic skill areas.

- Your school places a great deal of emphasis on measured student outcomes.

- Teachers use student assessment information to give feedback and plan instruction.

- The principal requires instructional plans from teachers and monitors them.

- Analysis and discussion of test content are part of the periodic curricular reviews.

- Assessment procedures are insufficient for evaluating student progress at our school.

Items such as these can be modified to survey different audiences including parents or students. As "frequent monitoring followed by adjustment" suggests, the key to this correlate is to monitor change over time on the dimensions the school leaders have chosen to use in their survey efforts.

Self-Report Questions

Data that inform the "adjust" portion of the monitor-and-adjust principle are the most useful in assessing implementation of this correlate. Self reports can identify students who began the school year performing at or above grade-level standards and adjustments the teachers are making most frequently (and for whom).

For example, if teachers determine that the monitoring reveals that some students routinely have difficulty on the assessments due to problems with vocabulary, the school might want to implement a preventative tutoring program. This program would focus on helping students learn new vocabulary before it is formally introduced in forthcoming lessons.

Self-report tools can be designed to promote adjustments by the teacher for individual students, small groups of students, the whole class, or even the curriculum frameworks. These tools could also be used to find out how well parents understand the performance feedback that they receive about their children. Finally, secondary students could provide useful insights about teacher-made tests if they were routinely asked to indicate whether there were items on the test that they did not expect, items that did not appear that they did expect, and which items they found most challenging. Such feedback from students, coupled with the item analysis of the test, would help classroom teachers become better test developers, something that is not easily accomplished.

Third-Party Direct Observations

A third-party observer of the monitoring process can perform much like the assistant football coach who is in the press box watching a game. This individual has a very different vantage point than the head coach on the sidelines and may see things the coach may miss. Similarly, during an assessment session, a third-party observer may be able to see things that might impact student performance (positively or negatively) that the teacher might miss. For example, an observer might offer information about the students' test-taking behaviors that indicate whether students appeared anxious, took the assessment seriously, understood the instructions, and paced themselves appropriately. These observations are not about issues pertaining to the content of the assessment, but more about the students' test-taking skills and the test environment. Another example illustrates the importance of having disinterested parties observe students in a testing situation. A new principal in a low-SES, heavily Hispanic elementary school had been implementing an effective schools program and was sure that her students would show significant gains in their scores over the previous year's scores. She also knew that she and her teachers might be questioned regarding cheating if this were to happen. Anticipating the possibility of such charges, the principal recruited volunteers from the local business community to observe the assessment sessions. When questions were raised because the results did improve dramatically, these third-party observers were called to tell what they saw. You see, people who don't believe all kids can learn often assume that good results in these unexpected places are achieved because cheating occurred.

Conclusion

This correlate is an indicator of how we as educators walk the talk. We may espouse a learning-for-all mission, but if we haven't put a system in place that allows us to manage the learning mission for all students, the practical impact of the mission is null and void. It becomes just another nice idea.

CHAPTER 8

Safe and Orderly Environment

In the effective school, an orderly, purposeful, and businesslike atmosphere free from the threat of physical and emotional harm exists. The school culture and climate are conducive to teaching and learning.

Before one can even hope to have an effective school, the minimum requirements to qualify the school as an institution must be established and maintained. In a chaotic environment, principals can't lead, teachers can't teach, and students can't learn. Creating and maintaining a safe and orderly school may be thought of as a necessary, but not sufficient condition for an effective school. A safe and orderly environment provides the setting in which all other correlates of an effective school can be successfully implemented.

Creating and maintaining a safe and orderly school climate has been described as one of the easier correlates to put in place if the school's leadership can first establish and maintain two essential prerequisites.

First, *all* the adults (but especially the teachers) must commit to the proposition that, while at school, they are on duty all the time and everywhere. Areas in the school where students observe (or legitimately perceive) that teachers are not on duty are obvious places for trouble to occur. Astor, Meyer, & Behre (1999) noted that it is generally known that most incidents of violence in schools occur in what might be called public places (lavatories, commons areas, and school grounds). The disciplinary problems associated with the public places tend to be more evident in the middle grades and high schools. On the other hand, misbehaviors are less likely to be observed in individual classrooms where teachers are present and vigilant. These observations tend to be true for all levels of schooling. Why? One theory that has been found to be true in many schools is that teachers see themselves as responsible for the disciplinary climate in their classrooms. They see someone else—usually the administration—as responsible everywhere else in the school. While this division of labor may sound sensible, it doesn't work.

Second, all the adults (but especially the teachers) must to commit to the proposition that they will behave with consistency around the agreed-upon rules and regulations of the school.

Rules, regulations, and universal acceptance of these are necessary for the school to function effectively as a system. We have described a system as having a clear aim, being manageable, and enjoying broad-based commitment among the adults. One of the challenges for school leaders is to build this broad-based and shared commitment. Establishing schoolwide commitment means that the expected discipline is not just the desire of a few teachers but represents a cultural rule that pertains to and is supported by everyone—especially the teachers.

Of course, teachers—like all individuals—vary in their attitudes toward discipline. Short and Short (1987) identified a continuum of teacher attitudes about discipline. At one extreme are educators whose philosophy is custodial; they believe that children will learn in a well-ordered, highly structured setting that offers little accommodation for children's individual differences. At the other extreme are those whose philosophy is humanistic. These educators believe that students are intrinsically motivated, naturally positive, and able, with appropriate guidance, to problem solve. These differences in attitude toward discipline also influence teacher perceptions of what constitutes a behavior problem.

Individual interpretation of the rules creates problems. If custodial-minded teachers define tardiness one way and humanistic-minded teachers define tardiness another way, we can predict that the school will have a tardiness problem into perpetuity. Furthermore, the resulting problem will not likely remain as a tardiness problem. Over time the problem will likely escalate into what the philosopher John Rawls (1999) refers to as a "distributive justice" problem—this school isn't fair. Findings from the early research into effective schools revealed that effective schools didn't leave discipline in the hands of individual teachers, but had consistent expectations for behavior and discipline across the school (Gaddy, 1988). This research makes clear that teachers are not likely to meet the standards of fairness and consistency unless or until they first know the rules, and more importantly, are committed to enforcing those rules.

How many rules should a school have? Research is clear that it is better for a school to have a few rules evenly applied by all staff rather than to have many rules unevenly applied. The number of rules that a school should have depends on the adults, not the students. The students will learn all the rules for which they will be held accountable. Unfortunately, adults will tend to be indifferent to those rules to which they are not committed.

Safe and Orderly Environment as a Product of School Culture

Deal and Peterson (1999) have studied and written extensively about corporate cultures. They define organizational culture in two ways: (1) this is the way we do things here; and (2) this is not the way we do things here. These definitions can be appropriately applied to schools. The school's disciplinary climate or culture can be defined as "the way we do things in this school." To the extent that the rules and regulations of a school are held sacred by all the staff, the vast majority of students will embrace them as the values that define the community.

In Edgar Schein's book *Organizational Culture and Leadership* (2004), he offers a useful way for examining school culture as it exists or as one might want it to be. The schematic in table 8.1, which we designed based on Schein's description, illustrates his approach. The table shows the connections among three levels of organizational culture: artifacts, espoused values, and basic underlying assumptions.

Table 8.1: Organizational Culture and Leadership

Levels of Culture
Artifacts
Visible organizational structure and processes (hard to decipher)
Espoused Values
Strategies, goals, and philosophies (espoused justifications)
Basic Underlying Assumptions
Unconscious, taken-for-granted beliefs, perceptions, thoughts, and feelings (ultimate sources of values and action)

Schein identifies three levels of organizational culture. The first level of culture focuses on the observable processes or structures. The second level of organizational culture is revealed when stakeholders are asked to indicate the presumed belief or value upon which the visible artifact rests. Once they articulate a belief, stakeholders often find the relationship between an artifact and their expressed values is not logical or realistic. For example, most elementary schools place students in learning groups based on their chronological age—an observable process. And yet, when viewed against the espoused value of learning for all, placing students in groups on the basis of age alone makes little sense. The third level of culture is revealed when we truly address the underlying assumptions and take actions that are consistent with our beliefs and assumptions.

Schein's framework is a very useful tool for creating the conversations needed to build a coherent, safe, and orderly school culture. Schein reminds us that deep change occurs at the third level of culture—the beliefs and values level of the organization. Strong and effective leadership is needed to foster change at this level.

An Expanded Interpretation of Safe and Orderly Environment

At one time, the safe and orderly environment correlate was defined as the absence of undesirable student behavior (such as fighting). As effective schools research evolved, the meaning of this correlate moved beyond rules and disciplinary practices, locker searches and security guards, to creating a cooperative, nurturing environment with a strong, academic focus. This shift in meaning reveals how the safe and orderly environment correlate intersects with the others: high expectations for success, strong instructional leadership, clear and focused mission, and frequent monitoring of student progress. Taken together, these correlates serve to create and sustain a culture of respect, academic achievement, and belonging.

Researcher Bob Sullo, author of *Activating the Desire to Learn* (2007), supports this interpretation of the correlate. In his book, he discusses the concept of internal control psychology. This concept is grounded in the idea that people are internally motivated to behave in specific ways to meet four basic psychological needs gleaned from the research of William Glasser: connecting, power or competence, freedom, and fun. Sullo asserts that most classrooms and schools operate on the opposite theory, that students are motivated by extrinsic rewards. In keeping with that philosophy, teacher-training programs instruct teachers on how to systematically reward and punish students. Thus, educators see themselves as shapers of student behavior through extrinsic rewards for compliant behavior. According to Sullo, this system of rewarding students for academic achievement sends the wrong message about the value of learning.

Sullo suggests that schools must find ways to motivate students by addressing the four psychological needs. Building a sense of community within the school fosters the students' need to belong. Enabling students to master academic material and offering them choices over what they learn helps to fulfill their needs for power and freedom. Making learning fun boosts student engagement and motivation. Through his qualitative research, Sullo found that schools employing this concept of internal control psychology have fewer disruptive student behaviors and students who do better academically.

The upshot of this research is that a safe and orderly environment is more than the absence of disruptive behavior. Schools must transform themselves into learning communities in which educators create need-satisfying environments. When students and teachers create a shared vision of what is to be learned, students are internally motivated to engage in high-quality academic work. Consequently, the reward-punishment mentality is diminished and the need for coercive discipline is severely reduced. Behavioral problems decrease and achievement increases.

Positive School Culture and Achievement

The effective schools research is replete with studies connecting a positive school culture and higher student achievement. Tschannen-Moran, Parish, and DiPaulo (2006) found that three attributes of school culture—(1) teacher professionalism, (2) academic press, and (3) community engagement—were directly related to student achievement in English and math. Of the three, two (academic press and community engagement) were directly related to achievement in writing. *Academic press* is defined as the overall tone of the school as a serious, orderly, and focused learning environment. There is a common spirit of pursuing excellence, high expectations of self and others, collaboration, and hard work.

Schools have gone about creating such a culture in many ways. Some have created small schools or learning communities within larger schools. The results for this strategy have been mixed. Schools that have been successful did more than downsize the learning environment. They capitalized on having fewer students by creating more personalized relationships between teachers and students and developing organizational structures to support students' academic and nonacademic needs. The most successful small schools embraced the push factor (academic press), highlighted by adult behaviors that challenged, stretched, and motivated students. Schools that downsized but don't foster a positive school culture ended up with students who felt isolated, powerless, and disengaged (Rodriquez, 2008).

In an effort to identify the disciplinary approaches of successful schools, Karin Chenoweth (2007) looked at fifteen schools that had significant numbers of students of color, low-income students, or both. Many differences between the schools were revealed in terms of facilities, parent and community involvement, calendars, district support, and school improvement models, ranging from prepackaged to self-developed ones. Despite these differences, the schools all had either very high rates of student academic proficiency or an impressive pace of improvement. Chenoweth found that these schools minimized the necessity for traditional discipline by incorporating schoolwide behavior expectations that focused on good behavior and productive use of time for instruction, leaving little time for discipline problems to develop. All the schools also shared a key underlying value: respect, for both the students and the adults within the school.

Safe and Orderly Environment in Action

Context matters. The organizational setting in which students are expected to learn can serve to either enhance or impede student learning. Optimal learning environments tend to be organized and relatively calm. When classrooms or schools are chaotic, even well-motivated learners struggle to maintain the focus demanded by the learning task. Contrary to the claims made by young people who say they can concentrate while listing to their iPod or watching TV, the evidence does not support this claim. The following sections highlight issues and strategies associated with this correlate.

Safe and Orderly Environment and Leadership

The principal plays a key role in developing a safe and orderly environment for a school. How the principal does this will vary from school to school, but the research is clear: the schools that are most successful in creating a safe and orderly environment and a positive school culture have a principal who promotes collaboration and collegiality among the staff (Brown & Anfara, 2002). The leader plays a critical role in empowering staff to identify discipline problems and develop strategies for dealing with them. When staff members are involved from the start, they are more eager to implement their strategies and more committed to seeing them through. Leaders also set a tone of respect for, and cooperation with, all members of the learning community (teachers, students, parents, and the community) (Rickert, 2005). Effective leaders use strategies to rid their environments of inappropriate student and staff behaviors by creating an environment that is trusting, supportive, and free of fear (Theoharis, 2007).

Horner, Sugai, and Horner (2000) identified six administrative traps that leaders can fall into when trying to create a safe and orderly environment:

1. Thinking that getting tough is enough
2. Focusing on the difficult few
3. Looking for a quick fix
4. Finding one powerful trick, like school uniforms or camera surveillance
5. Believing someone else has the solution
6. Believing more procedures are better

To avoid these traps, administrators should emphasize prevention by establishing a culture of learning and respect and providing quick, efficient, and effective supports for problem behaviors.

Effective leaders who create safe and orderly schools not only concentrate on the big picture of school culture, but also make sure that every teacher's classroom culture reflects the common vision of learning for all, respect, and collaboration. Since teachers control classroom cultures, the leader must make sure that all staff not only understand the vision, but that they also know what the vision looks like in practice and have the necessary training to be able to implement strategies that will create a positive learning environment free of disciplinary distractions (Finnan, Schnepel, & Anderson, 2003).

Practitioner Perspectives and Insights

In keeping with our practice of surveying practitioners for their perspectives and insights about the correlates, in the late spring of 2009 we conducted a Reality Check online perceptual survey focused on the correlate of safe and orderly environment. This survey included items about the threat of physical harm in the school, sources of threats to safety and orderliness in school, frequency of disciplinary measures in the school, and policies that could increase safety and orderliness in school. Four hundred and seventeen educators responded to the survey. Of these, 47 percent of respondents indicated they worked in the elementary setting. Approximately equal percentages of respondents indicated that they worked in a middle school (15 percent), a high school (19 percent), or the central office and other (19 percent).

The results of this survey included good news about the school environment. Eighty-nine percent of the respondents indicated that they agreed or strongly agreed that the vast majority of students and staff perceive the school is free from the threat of physical harm. In addressing the disciplinary problems that did exist in their schools, the majority of respondents (99 percent) reported that less than 15 percent of the students created most of the disciplinary problems. In fact, 78 percent of the respondents indicated that fewer than 5 percent of the students created most of the disciplinary problems.

The item about the single greatest threat to safety and orderliness in schools today prompted a wide range of responses from 390 participants in the survey. The majority of the respondents indicated that the greatest threat to safety in the schools comes from outside the schools. Home and family situations were cited most frequently. Larger societal and community issues were also listed frequently among the out-of-school factors. These societal issues often take the form of drugs, gangs, bullying, and harassment.

Respondents identified factors within the school and district that threaten safety and orderliness. Lack of effective district policies and programs were noted relatively frequently. In addition, several respondents indicated that ineffective instruction and inconsistent application of the rules contributed to threats to safety and orderliness. However, the largest number of respondents viewed the lack of parental support as the greatest threat.

Three hundred ninety-nine individuals responded to the item about disciplinary offenses that occur most frequently in their schools. The most frequent responses centered on bullying, verbal harassment, fighting, and similar offenses between and among the students. In addition, respondents identified other examples of discipline problems including students showing defiance and disrespect, and verbal confrontations between students and adults. A small percentage of the respondents mentioned classroom disruptions, truancy, and other off-task distractions as further examples of frequent disciplinary offenses.

As part of this survey, 356 people offered suggestions for policies that could increase the safety and orderliness of the schools. The responses to this question were much more diverse than those on most other questions, ranging from observations that focused directly on classrooms to those that suggested general ideas (such as more engaging instruction, and rewarding and recognizing positive behaviors).

Some respondents suggested that schools develop closer partnerships with parents, especially for troubled students. Some of the respondents wanted to go easier on students (for example, fewer suspensions) while others wanted schools to be tougher on misbehaving students. Some respondents wanted to create dress codes and others wanted to eliminate them.

Several respondents suggested that schools need to make sure teachers are committed to the notion that they are on duty, everywhere, all the time. Some noted that teachers must model the respect they seek. A sprinkling of suggestions included requiring name badges, securing the building, and training the playground supervisors.

It seems that there were as many different (sometime contradictory) suggestions as to how to best create and maintain a safe and orderly school environment as there were respondents. While all the respondents seemed to recognize the importance of this dimension of school life, they were not at all clear about how best to create a school climate conducive to learning.

Another item sought observations about the link between school climate and the learning mission of the school. Three hundred ninety-three individuals responded to this question: "What do you consider to be the key to establishing and maintaining a positive school climate that supports the learning mission of the school?" The most frequent responses fit into what we call the "C category:" communication, collaboration, caring, cooperation, and consistency. Other suggestions that supported the learning mission included high and clear expectations, strong leadership, effective classroom instruction all the time, and a commitment to a clear school philosophy and shared values. Surprisingly, given the responses to earlier questions, working toward an effective partnership with parents was suggested by only a few participants. There was also some support for showing respect for students and their parents, along with the importance of positive attitudes.

Research-Supported Strategies

Researchers have long been interested in studying factors that contribute to a school culture that is positive and conducive to effective teaching and learning. Findings from selected studies are summarized in this section:

Take a positive approach to disciplinary issues. Utilizing a leadership team, the principal of an Oregon school overrun with disciplinary problems involved all staff in identifying areas of disciplinary concern. Tardiness and loitering in the halls topped the list. Instead of resorting to negative sanctions—suspensions and detentions—the staff instituted a process called the "sweep." In this process, when teachers designated as "sweepers" found students lingering in the hallways, they would help students get ready for class and escort them to the classroom so they would arrive on time. The program launched in the fall and began with an orientation for students. During this orientation, students learned about the importance of the first fifteen minutes of class. Staff explained that, during this initial class time, teachers usually explained what the class was about and what would be required of the students. The staff also explained the sweep to the students, what they could expect from the sweeper, and what the sweeper would expect from them. When sweepers found students in the hall, they didn't scold students, but took a positive approach, calmly reminding students why it was important to get to class on time, chatting with them, and praising those who improved. This program decreased disciplinary referrals from 6,007 to 2,078 in one year; by the second year, referrals fell to 850, an 85 percent reduction (Rickert, 2005).

Institute common lunch periods. One high school of nearly 2,000 students switched to a single, common fifty-minute lunch period for all students. After working through some initial resistance and logistical problems, the revised schedule became widely accepted and continued to be popular with staff and students several years later, and the suspension rate dropped from 19 percent to 5.4 percent. Student achievement rose dramatically, and surveys of students, staff, and parents were predominantly positive. Staff reported improved collegiality and planning opportunities (Goodman, 2006).

Increase a sense of community. A California school divided itself into social "houses" as a means of building school community. Each house reflected the diversity of the school and included students of various races, ethnicities, ages, and academic abilities. All faculty and staff were also assigned to a house. Students named each house and helped select a house logo. Students attended classes as usual during the regular school day, but they also participated as members of a house during social and academic competitions, community service activities, and school leadership meetings. The house approach resulted in significant decreases in suspensions and bullying, as well as reported incidents of violence. In addition, there was a significant increase in achievement scores (Green, 2006).

Look at underlying factors of misbehavior. Students with chronic behavior problems often have physical, mental, or emotional conditions that severely limit their ability to learn. Cincinnati Public Schools created the Project Succeed Academy (PSA) for students who struggled academically, behaviorally, and socially. The program was designed to provide academic support in all subjects, as well as health and wellness and case management. Staff members received classroom-embedded professional development on a regular basis so they could learn how to work effectively with students with behavior problems. During PSA's first full year of implementation, the district recorded a 23 percent drop in suspensions and a 12 percent drop in expulsions. In the second year, records for those infractions showed an additional 11 percent and 8 percent drop, respectively (Brown, 2004).

Remember that teachers are key. Marzano and Marzano (2003) found that the teacher-student relationship is key to all other aspects of classroom management, and that teachers who had good relationships with their students experienced 30 percent fewer discipline problems. The researchers identified three essential teacher behaviors for maintaining effective discipline: appropriate levels of teacher dominance, appropriate levels of cooperation, and awareness of high-needs students.

Be visible. One study found that as administrator visibility in junior high classrooms increased, the number of disciplinary detentions and referrals decreased significantly (Keesor, 2005). For those administrators who say they don't have time to visit classrooms, this study found that a classroom visit took fifteen minutes, while each student referral took forty-five minutes.

Know that the physical environment matters. Plank, Bradshaw, and Young (2009) found that physical disorder of the school was strongly related to the amount of social disorder, fearfulness, and the collective efficacy of the staff. Poor maintenance sends a message that nobody really cares about the school building, and by association, the students and the learning mission. The researchers found that when the students and staff of the school perceived the physical plant of the school to be in poor condition, the resulting increased levels of fear and alienation were perceived to "disrupt teaching, learning and healthy adolescent development" (p. 243). Schools and school leaders should work with policymakers and decision makers to establish short- and long-term preventative facility maintenance programs; these programs will ensure that physical order variables do not adversely impact the social order of the learning environment. In a time of unprecedented fiscal challenges, schools and school systems may be hard pressed to use valuable resources on the aesthetic and physical needs of the learning environment. However, in this study, researchers Plank, Bradshaw, and Young provide strong justification and rationale for doing so.

Developing a Data Dashboard

As we have noted in our descriptions of monitoring the other correlates, perception, to a great extent, is in the eye of the beholder. Two individuals can look at the same reality, and because they bring different experiential lenses to the situation, they see things differently and draw different conclusions. The extent to which a school is perceived to exemplify a safe, orderly, businesslike atmosphere will vary depending on whom one asks. Nonetheless, school leaders need to create and maintain measurement tools that provide credible information from all stakeholders about indicators relevant to implementation of the correlate. The basic tools, perceptual surveys, self reports, and third-party direct observations for measuring the correlates remain useful for school leaders and leadership teams to track progress and address challenges in implementing the safe and orderly environment correlate. For purposes of monitoring this correlate, we include an additional section—"Data Collected for a Different Purpose." For example, schools are required by their states to report on students who are suspended or expelled for various readings. These data can be used to track changes in the level of safety and orderliness of the school over time.

Safe and orderly environment measures present a special challenge to educational leaders. In times past, educators could assume that the vast majority of the community formulated their opinions about their schools by looking over the shoulders of their own children or the neighbors' children. This is changing, and many individuals' views of public schools are influenced by other factors. Family structures and social networks have become far more diverse in recent decades, and neighborhoods far less homogeneous. There is less free time, and people interact with their neighbors far less than previous generations. There are fewer children overall, and the ability of the media to instantaneously (and relentlessly) cover negative school events and poor test scores has expanded exponentially. These factors influence the public's views of local schools even though the information they receive may be based on incidents outside the local school and district. For example, an evening news report on a violent incident that occurred in school a thousand miles away can negatively influence how community members view their own schools. Since something that is perceived as real is real in its consequences, such media coverage can undermine a community's confidence in its own schools. It is extremely important for all schools to develop, assess, and report the facts when it comes to student and staff safety. For this reason, we explain data that are collected to inform the public.

Perceptual Survey Questions

Individual surveys administered anonymously can provide important details about the school climate. Teachers, other school staff, and students and their parents—the individuals most directly involved with the correlates—should be surveyed on a regular basis. The successful implementation of the correlates depends on their participation, so their responses should be more informative and carry more weight. Members of the general community can be surveyed less often.

Reality Check includes 344 items designed to assess the disciplinary climate of the school. The items are organized in three subcategories: (1) general school climate and student behavior, (2) the physical plant of the school, and (3) student discipline. The following examples suggest some survey items that can be used to assess and monitor the school's disciplinary climate. Ask respondents to indicate their level of agreement (strongly agree, agree, undecided, disagree, strongly disagree, or not applicable) regarding statements such as:

- I feel safe when I'm at school.
- Teachers at this school really care about the students.
- Teachers at this school treat all students fairly and consistently.
- Our school's physical plant is a source of school pride.
- All stakeholders know the acceptable student behaviors and expect those who violate them to be sanctioned.
- Discipline is not a problem in our school.

Self-Report Questions

It is axiomatic that the classroom is the primary locus of student learning. Therefore, any problems associated with the disciplinary climate in classrooms take a toll on the learning of all students in the classroom, and may even affect behavior throughout the entire school. School leaders and leadership teams should develop a small number of classroom-level self-report items that are collected and monitored over time. These indicators can be designed to answer the basic journalistic questions: who is involved in what kinds of infractions, and where, when, and how do they disrupt the classroom learning? These reports, assembled over time, will reveal the source and nature of the discipline problems. Many of the disciplinary infractions that occur in classrooms are attributed to poor instruction and poor classroom management practices.

Data from the self reports will help identify those teachers who seem to be struggling with classroom discipline issues and those who seem to be more effective in setting a positive learning climate in their classroom. It follows that the teachers who need help can benefit from mentoring sessions with the effective teachers. The data represent the key to positive collaboration—otherwise the discussion may turn out to be divisive and unproductive.

Third-Party Direct Observations

Classrooms where students are actively and productively engaged tend to be classrooms with positive disciplinary climates. Therefore, school leaders should focus on variables that monitor student engagement. Unfortunately, there are real limits on the specificity of the data that can be constructed (self reported) by the teachers. A third party in the school and classroom can be much more focused and much more intentional when looking at indicators that are associated with the disciplinary climate of the school and its classrooms.

In the previous chapter that examined opportunity to learn and time on task, we wrote about conducting classroom observations to calculate the levels of student engagement during different subjects, times of the day, or days of the week. Because of the interactive relationship between student engagement and the classroom disciplinary climate, this type of indicator can serve several important elements that define the effective school and classrooms.

A third-party observer can also inform many other important school variables that are not associated with specific in-classroom behaviors. For example, researchers have reported that most discipline problems in secondary schools occur in what are called public places in the school. Some of the obvious public places include hallways, stairwells, commons areas, rest rooms, and so on. A third-party observer could be tasked to conduct observations and make recordings of the events that are associated with disruptive behaviors in some of these public places. For example, suppose the observer documents the number and frequency of student problems associated with certain school halls during the passing of classes. Next, suppose the school leadership team takes action and has teachers stand outside their classroom doors during the passing of classes. The observer would be able to answer the question: has the incidence of negative behaviors decreased as a result of this intervention?

The possible uses of a third-party observer in schools and classrooms are virtually limitless and can be customized to the needs of the school and its classrooms. It is amazing how access to credible data about issues and concerns can change the nature and tone of conversation in a school staff. Sometimes the best way to solve a problem that is detracting from the mission of learning is to "make the familiar strange."

Data Collected for a Different Purpose

Parents care about the safety of their children and want to know that the disciplinary climate in the local school ensures their children will be safe. Schools are required to report on violent acts that have occurred in the school, incidents of threatened assault against staff and other students, and incidents of weapons brought on campus. Reports on the number of students that are suspended or expelled from the school are also required. Assessing and monitoring change over time and reporting the facts to the school and larger community provide evidence of the level of safety and order in the school.

Conclusion

The safe and orderly subsystem that defines a school's climate or culture cannot be set in place and left to remain static. The larger society is constantly changing. Educators cannot ignore these changes, some of which have implications for codes of behavior expected in school. The rules and regulations that define the disciplinary climate of the school have to be reinterpreted from time to time. For example, the availability and use of cell phones in the school and classroom is one of the challenges high schools confront today. Even a few years ago, cell phones were not a matter of concern for educators. Today cell phones are ubiquitous—especially for high school students. Generally, it is considered reasonable for students to have cell phones with them at school. Parents and their children want to be able to contact each other on a moment's notice in the event of an emergency. However, some students abuse the cell phone privilege by using the technology to cheat on tests or harass other students. Text messaging is a relatively new challenge that school leaders must confront in their aim to create a safe and orderly school environment. The impact of technology is only one source of change that can affect the school environment. Staff must be vigilant to ensure that the safe and orderly environment is maintained in spite of changing conditions either within or outside of the school.

CHAPTER 9

Positive Home-School Relations

In an effective school, parents and other members of the community are familiar with the school's mission, and the leadership provides a variety of opportunities for them to support the mission.

The positive home-school relations correlate is a logical follow-up to the description of the safe and orderly environment correlate in the previous chapter. While it is true that parents and educators care deeply about the academic core of the school, initially, they care about the host of factors that form the disciplinary climate of the school. Parents want to know that their children are in a safe and caring school environment. Likewise, teachers typically solicit parental help and support in the area of school and classroom discipline before they seek parental help with the academic core of the school. In many ways, the two correlates could be considered extensions of one another. They are presented separately because of the independent research support for each.

Like all the correlates, the positive home-school relations correlate is deceptively simple to describe, but unusually complex to execute across the diverse student groups that make up the demographics of the typical school. For example, when it comes to discipline, parents usually expect the school's staff to treat their children as the parents would treat them at home. In practice, the variability in parenting styles makes it nearly impossible for a school staff to know the types of action that individual parents prefer. What is a staff to do?

Parent involvement is filled with paradox. First, when the school has an open house, parents' night or parent-teacher conferences, the parents whose children need such partnerships the least are usually among the first to come. On the other hand, the parents whose children would benefit the most from a stronger home-school partnership often do not come at all. Similarly, stay-at-home moms and dads are better positioned to visit their children's classroom during school hours, whereas parents who work outside the home are limited in their ability to visit school at such times. These situations illustrate challenges educators encounter when seeking to build strong home-school relations, a necessary element in an effective school. Leaders of effective schools use a variety of strategies and provide many opportunities for parents and caregivers to be involved with their children's schooling in order to create a strong partnership that makes student success more likely. These leaders also recognize that the absence of desired parental support cannot be used as an excuse to give up on those students.

History of Parent Involvement in Schooling in the U. S.

Prior to the 1980s, there was little research and discussion of parent involvement in education. Children were sent to school, and formal school-parent communications were generally limited to report cards and periodic teacher-parent conferences. Middle-class families with stay-at-home moms had more interaction with schools, in the classroom, and organizationally in parent groups. As more and more mothers returned to the workforce in the 1970s and 1980s, parent involvement in schools declined. At the same time, student populations of most schools were becoming increasingly diverse, both culturally and linguistically. These factors have contributed to the difficulties schools face today in fostering a positive and productive relationship with parents.

Recognizing the importance of parent involvement in schooling, early Title I federal legislation in the United States established provisions for involving parents in their children's learning. No Child Left Behind took parent involvement a step further and specifically defined it as "the participation of parents in regular, two-way, and meaningful communication involving student academic learning and other school activities" (U.S. Department of Education, 2004). Under this law, schools receiving Title I funding were required to adopt specific strategies for involving parents in their children's schooling, including parents who traditionally had not participated with the schools due to cultural, language, socioeconomic, or other barriers. For example, schools and districts with large numbers of English learners have been required to offer written school policies in the students' home languages. NCLB has made it clear that building the capacity of parents to be involved in their children's education was a priority by requiring schools and districts to spend a significant portion of their Title I dollars on doing just that.

The school-parent compact is another sign of the importance attached to parent involvement in schools. Developed initially in 1994 as one of the Title I requirements and subsequently reinforced and expanded under NCLB, the compact defines the expectations and promises of both the school's and parents' responsibilities. While schools are required to develop the document, parents are asked—but not required—to sign the compact as evidence of their awareness and support. The school-parent compact is intended to set the stage for mutual understanding and provide a basis for ongoing communication between the school and parents of children attending the school.

The Importance of Parent Involvement

Decades of research have shown the value of parent involvement, revealing a consistent, positive relationship between parents' engagement in their children's education and student outcomes. In an in-depth review of this research, Henderson and Mapp (2002) offered many important insights into the effects of parent involvement. They found that students whose parents were involved with their schooling, regardless of their income or background, were more likely to earn higher grades and test scores, enroll in higher-level programs, pass their classes, and earn credits. These students also attended school more regularly, exhibited better social skills and school behavior, and were more likely to graduate and go on to postsecondary education.

William Jeynes (2005) concurred with these findings in his meta-analysis of 41 studies related to parent involvement and urban elementary schools. Specifically, he found that parent involvement in schooling, both directly with their child and through school-sponsored programs, had a significant, positive impact on student achievement. This relationship held true regardless of race, socioeconomic status, or gender.

The Elements of Parent Involvement

Joyce Epstein and her colleagues (2002), noted researchers on parent-school relations, developed a framework for six types of parent involvement in the child's education. The six types of involvement are:

1. Parenting (providing such basics as food and shelter)
2. Communicating (primarily school-initiated)
3. Volunteering
4. Learning at home (for example, help with homework or exposure to such outside learning as museums)
5. Decision making (family participation in school governance and advocacy)
6. Collaborating with the community

Epstein found that learning at home was the most significant factor in student achievement. In his 2007 study of urban secondary schools, William Jeynes used similar variables in his analysis of parent involvement: parental expectations of the student's ability to achieve at a high level; parental attendance and participation in school functions and activities; communication between parents and their children about school matters; parents' checking homework regularly; and parental ability to maintain an adequate level of discipline while being loving and supportive.

The results of Jeynes' later analysis (2007) were consistent with his 2005 study—that parent involvement had a significant effect on student achievement, whether initiated by the parent or the school. While each element of parent involvement had a positive effect on student achievement, Jeynes found that parent expectations exerted the most influence over student achievement, while parent attendance at school events and consistent rules at home had the smallest effect.

Issues in Parent Involvement

While generalizations are always tricky, it is generally true that levels of parental support are stronger with elementary students (Sheldon & Van Voorhis, 2004). As students progress to middle or high school, parental partnership in pursuit of the school mission is more difficult to achieve and maintain. Schools with high concentrations of minority or low-income students, as well as those with a significant number of English learners, also have lower levels of parent involvement, as well as lower educational expectations of their children (Lee & Bowen, 2006). Many reasons account for the lack of parent involvement among these groups. Sanders, Allen-Jones, and Abel (2002) found that many of these parents feel unwelcome because of their own educational experiences, feel culturally out of sync with the school staff, or have work schedules that prohibit active participation in school activities. Many of these parents simply don't know what to do to help their children with learning because they struggle with their own educational deficits or difficulties with English.

Home-School Relations and the Community

Factors in the community where children live can influence home-school relations. Research has shown that poor children enter the educational system approximately two years behind their more affluent counterparts on various measures of school readiness (Knitzer & Lefkowitz, 2006). From that day forward, educators spend the next twelve years trying to close that gap, making efforts to ensure that all students master a high-standards curriculum. Smart self-interest suggests that if educators could somehow reduce or even eliminate the achievement gap before kindergarten, these students' journeys to curriculum mastery would be more attainable. Like poverty itself, the incidence of vulnerable infants and toddlers is not evenly distributed across all communities and school districts. Some districts may even naïvely believe that poverty is not an issue for them. One way to test this theory is to ask kindergarten teachers whether they believe that all children, especially the children of poverty, enter kindergarten ready for school. Call collect if all the kindergarten teachers answer "Yes!" Indeed, they are working in a rare district!

Systems scholars know that the most cost-effective solution to most problems is to prevent them, if possible, at the outset. Clearly, early intervention can help to reduce (if not eliminate) the downstream learning problems these most vulnerable children experience. Some observers say that the problems of these children are not and should not be the schools' problem. On one level, the observers are right. The schools' outreach is limited in dealing with such issues as maternal and infant health and child socialization in the preschool years. However, when these children arrive in kindergarten or first grade, the school becomes responsible for their learning and must deal with the attendant problems the children bring. Because the schools alone cannot deal with these demands, they must enter into strategic alliances with a wide range of agencies and organizations that serve the most vulnerable children and their families.

When educational resources are already tight, what can financially strapped schools bring to the table that would help these institutions and the children and families they serve? First, the school physical plant may be the best setting for the service providers and recipients to connect. Second, most social service providers are reactive; families must find them to access the service. Teachers could help these institutions become more proactive by making referrals since they often have information about a family before any other service providers. Effective parenting programs could be jointly developed and offered by schools in partnership with other agencies and institutions. If educators and social services personnel are able to work together to help parents be more effective in those early years, significant benefits will result for families, children, and teachers in the later years in school.

Positive Home-School Relations in Action

Trust is a longstanding cornerstone of the relationship between parents and schools. When there is a strong and positive partnership between all parties, student learning is enhanced. On the other hand, for many different reasons, when the trust and communication between the partners breaks down, learning is negatively impacted. In this case, fixing blame tends to take precedence over fixing the problem.

Leadership and Positive Home-School Relations

The effective schools movement has traditionally advocated the involvement of parents in their children's education; however, the specifics of how parents should be involved have been somewhat unclear. Furthermore, educators have often shown mixed attitudes toward parent involvement. Some teachers and principals want parents to be involved only to the extent to which the educators can feel comfortable. Parents who are perceived as overinvolved and critical are considered a nuisance or even a threat to teachers (Hassrick & Schneider, 2009). Other parents are not sufficiently involved, and that is a source of concern to educators. Parents whose cultural and linguistic attributes distance them from the school, combined with a school that disregards the importance of parent involvement, can create a climate of mistrust that suppresses parent involvement even more.

The school leader is responsible for helping teachers and parents confront the issue of parent involvement—not each other—in a way that builds trust and understanding. The leader must create a school climate that fosters an authentic partnership between teachers and parents, and the realization that every member of the school community has the same goal: a quality education and a successful future for every child.

Practitioner Perspectives and Insights

We conducted a Reality Check online survey about the positive home-school relations correlate in the late spring of 2009. The survey invited practitioners to share their perceptions on several aspects of this correlate: number of parents who could be relied on to help their children at home with schoolwork; historical perspective on change in the level of parent involvement; extent to which parents of children who need help are involved; number of parents who attend invited events at school; extent to which the school or district encourages parent visits while school is in session; parent membership on the school's improvement leadership team; and trends in the strength of the home-school partnership. Respondents were asked to indicate their level of agreement with the survey statements. The survey also asked practitioners to describe programs, policies, or procedures that fostered positive home-school relations.

Two hundred seven educators responded to the survey. Half of the respondents identified themselves with the elementary school level and relatively equal percentages of individuals indentified themselves with middle grades (18 percent), high school (13 percent), and central office (19 percent).

The practitioners were asked to indicate what percent of parents could be counted on to provide help and support at home for their children on school-related activities. The majority (65 percent) of respondents felt that only about half or less of the parents could be counted upon to provide help. If this is accurate, teachers find themselves in a tough spot when it comes to assignments that must be completed outside of school. The lack of parental support could turn out to be an achievement gap "builder," not a "closer."

When asked to put the issue of parental support in a historical context, the conclusion is even more troublesome. Respondents were asked to indicate whether the level of parental support has changed in recent years. Eleven percent indicated that the level of parental support had increased, 27 percent indicated that it had remained about the same, and 60 percent thought it had decreased. Throughout the history of universal public education, there have always been parents who have failed in supporting their children's schoolwork. However, if our practitioner estimates are correct and only half of the parents can be counted on (and the trend suggests that the number of parents who cannot be counted on is increasing), educators face a real dilemma when it comes to ensuring that all students master a high-standards curriculum while at the same time closing the achievement gap.

Respondents were then asked to comment on whether their experience suggested that the parents of children who need the most help and support are the same parents who cannot be counted on to provide it. One hundred ninety-three respondents responded. Approximately 60 percent indicated that, for them, the statement was true or very true. About 20 percent indicated that they did not agree with the statement. The remaining 20 percent indicated that while the statement was generally true, they believed parents actually do support education but lack either the skills or the necessary time to actually provide it.

The respondents were asked to indicate, based on their personal experience, what percent of parents tend to come to invited events (parent-teacher conferences, open houses, school programs, and so on). Sixty percent of respondents indicated that at least half or more of the parents tend to come to such events. Approximately 30 percent indicated that three-quarters or more parents tend to come to such events. Nineteen percent indicated that the percent of parents that attend invited events had increased in recent years, half of the respondents indicated that the percentage has remained about the same in recent years, and 31 percent indicated that the number of parents attending invited events had decreased.

Fifty-nine percent of the respondents indicated that their school or district encourages parents to make classroom visits while school is in session. The remaining 41 percent indicated that their school or district does not encourage such visits. Most of the respondents who say their school encourages visits indicated that less than half of the parents actually make at least one classroom visit a year. In a few cases, the respondents indicated that 60 to 75 percent of their students' parents make a classroom visit while school is in session.

When asked whether their schools have parent members on their school improvement leadership teams, 55 percent indicated that they always have parent members, and 27 percent indicated "sometimes." Only about 17 percent said they seldom or never have parent members on the school leadership teams.

A total of 191 participants responded to the question, "Do you feel that the majority of teachers feel supported by the parents of the children in their classes when it comes to resolving academic or disciplinary problems involving their children?" Approximately 70 percent answered yes, while the remaining 30 percent responded no. Some said that while the overwhelming majority of the parents are supportive of the teachers, a small number are not; those unsupportive parents can make life extremely difficult and challenging for the teachers affected.

When asked to characterize the general trend when it comes to the strength of the partnership between home and school, the following responses were offered: 15 percent said that the partnership between home and school was strong and getting even stronger. Twenty-nine percent said that the partnership was generally strong and not changing much. Thirty-one percent said it was generally not strong and not changing much, and 21 percent said it was getting weaker over the last few years.

Another part of the survey asked practitioners to share any programs, policies, or district or school practices that they had found to be most effective in creating and maintaining high levels of parent involvement and support in their schools. A total of 182 practitioners responded with a wide variety of comments. Approximately 40 percent of the responses focused on using student-centered events, as well as more traditional activities like athletics, to keep parents invested as partners. A few respondents from the elementary level stressed the value of providing food at invited events to ensure a good turnout of the parents.

At a more abstract level, some of the respondents suggested that creating an organizational culture that focuses on openness and caring sets the tone for a strong partnership with the parents. A few commented on the desirability of encouraging many different parent organizations and many different ways in which parents can be involved (for example, parent members of school leadership teams).

The responses from practitioners on this survey revealed similarities with themes and strategies drawn from research studies that we summarize in the next section.

Research-Supported Strategies

Involve guidance staff in creating relationships with parents. One school district found that incorporating school counselors into the leadership teams improved parent-teacher relations by strengthening teacher capacity to work with parents and students more positively. The use of counselors also gave parents and students a more active role in schooling, reinforced each group's responsibility for student success, and created a dialogue with families about learning (Amatea & Vandiver, 2004).

Educate staff about struggling families and the challenges they face. An elementary school with 99 percent low-income students began its approach to parent involvement by educating the staff about the challenges low-income families face, and how the gap between low-income families and middle-class teachers could hinder parent involvement. Understanding the life circumstances of these families reduced the tendency for teachers to blame them when their students faced academic challenges (Smith, 2006).

Partner with the community. This same school created the Family Resource Center, partnering with government agencies, churches, community organizations, and businesses to bring needed programs and services for parents into the school. In addition to providing direct services and referrals, the Center offered other activities for parents, including family games, computers, and literacy classes. The Center became a place for parents not only to receive services, but also to meet other parents and begin to feel a sense of community within the school, and to gain confidence regarding their ability to positively influence their children's education (Smith, 2006).

Offer nonthreatening opportunities for parent involvement. A lending library for parents, placed in the main hallway of a preschool where a large number of children from low income and immigrant families were enrolled, proved to be a successful strategy for supporting and strengthening home literacy environments (Taylor & Pearson, 2004). For three years, 80 percent of the families were regular participants. The study showed a significant correlation between the length of time children participated in the book loan program and their scores on reading assessment tests. Parents' interest in books and their understanding of how to stimulate literacy at home increased as a result of their participation in the lending library.

Evaluate your parent outreach efforts. Sheldon and Van Voorhis (2004) found that one of the most important characteristics influencing the quality of school-parent partnership programs was the program evaluation process: "Schools and school districts that evaluated the progress of their partnership program reported higher-quality programs and fewer obstacles to their work, and conducted more district-level leadership activities" (p. 129). Onsite evaluation helped schools identify strengths, weaknesses, and areas for improvement, thereby increasing program quality over time. Based on findings from the study, the researchers concluded, "When action teams use evaluation tools to reflect on their plans, activities, successes, and failures, they are more likely to improve the design and conduct of partnership activities from one year to the next" (p. 141).

Use multiple and frequent forms of school-parent communication. Sheldon and Epstein (2002) found that the highest-rated practices for communicating with parents were using day planners or assignment books, conducting orientation sessions at the beginning of the school year for new families, and conducting parent workshops on school goals and behavioral expectations.

Anticipate that parent involvement may take extraordinary effort. Lam (2004) chronicled his efforts to involve the parents of his primarily poor, Hispanic class in passing their New York state exams. Of his twenty-four students, only three had passed the previous year's state exams in reading and math. He made Herculean efforts to establish a relationship with every parent, and involved them in test preparation workshops as students worked toward taking the state tests. His efforts were rewarded with 57 percent of students passing the English arts test and 74 percent passing the math test. In 2003, over 90 percent of his students passed the tests.

Offer learning resources to parents as well as their children. Research has shown that involving parents who are not proficient in English and from varying ethnic backgrounds can be very difficult. The typical school setting can be very intimidating for these parents and their cultural traditions may discourage close interaction with the school. The New Jersey Red Bank Borough School System, with 44 percent Hispanic students, addressed this disconnect with a nonthreatening approach to involving parents with their children. The district created an after-school program that featured two computer-based programs: Skills Tutor, that would allow students to work on academic areas, and English Discoveries, that was appropriate for both parents and students for whom English was a second language. Through this program, parents improved their English and thus their communication with instructors, and became more comfortable with the school setting and with computer technology. The program also provided an avenue for these parents to be involved with their students' schooling (McCurry & Krewer, 2003).

Reach out systematically. Taylor and Pearson (2004) found that in the more successful schools, teachers and administrators reached out to parents frequently and systematically, recruited volunteers from the community to help in the classroom, and made great efforts to extend literacy into all homes using diverse methods.

Developing a Data Dashboard

School leaders constantly strive to maintain positive relationships with the community generally and the parents of the students specifically. Educators believe, at a deep level, that the education of a child is going to be more successful if the educators and the child's "emotionally significant others" work together as a partnership. Further, educational leaders know that to create and maintain the desired relationship, open, honest communication and high levels of trust must exist on all sides.

Positive home-school relations can be damaged if the actions of either partner are based on assumptions and not informed by data. If ignored, two potential pitfalls can derail home-school relations. The first pitfall is on the educator's side of the partnership. Substantial variability exists among teachers in the openness, warmth, and trust they show as they interact with the parents of their students. Some teachers show warmth and an authentic level of caring that provides comfort and reassurance to the parents. Other teachers are not so inclined and are more distant in their contacts with parents. Because of this inevitable variability, many different levels of home-school relations may be evident in schools. Right or wrong, fair or unfair, parents, based on their experiences in the school, often generalize from specific encounters in the classroom to the entire school. Depending on the nature of their experiences, their generalizations can have either positive or negative consequences for the entire staff. Ongoing assessment of the home-school relationship will help ensure that potential negative or damaged relations are prevented, avoided, or eliminated.

The second pitfall that can derail home-school relations is the mirror image of the first problem and can be found on the parents' side of the partnership. Parents may approach the school and the teachers of their children with a mindset based on their own experiences with schools and teachers. Sometimes the mindset leans toward the positive, and the educators are seen as trusted partners until the interactions prove otherwise. On the other hand, parents sometimes bring a mindset of distrust and suspicion to the relationship. Consequently, teachers are sometimes inclined to generalize from these differing contacts and begin to see all parents as either trusting or distrusting. To avoid this pitfall, school leaders need to collect, analyze, and discuss credible data regarding the trust levels that exist between teachers and parents.

Perceptual surveys, self reports, and third-party direct observations can serve to guide school leaders in developing a data dashboard for assessing and monitoring the home-school partnership from both sides of the relationship. We also include "Data Collected for a Different Purpose" with the assessment tools for use with this correlate. No single set of measures can be expected to reveal the whole story, so it is necessary for school leaders to customize the tools for their context (taking into account the school's history and current status). For example, teachers in urban schools and schools that serve concentrated populations of poor and minority students often struggle to increase the level of parent involvement and support. On the other hand, teachers in schools serving concentrated populations of middle-class and upper-class advantaged students may believe that, even with parent involvement, you can have too much of good thing.

Data Collected for a Different Purpose

From the first time parents register their children for school and throughout the years the children remain in the school, there are many opportunities for home and school communication. For example, selected items currently on the school registration form could serve to tap parent attitudes and expectations regarding schools and teachers. Schools routinely keep a record of the number and percent of the parents who attend open houses, parent-teacher conferences, and student-centered events. Data from these records can be used, perhaps with minor modifications, to inform the ongoing health of the home-school partnership.

Teachers also have various communications that can be used to assess the general level of responsiveness of parents. Examples include established routines where the parents are asked to sign off on student assignments, or to sign and return report cards and class or school newsletters. School leaders should select a few indicators that best reflect the schoolwide emphasis required to monitor change in parental attitudes and behaviors over time.

Perceptual Survey Questions

Reality Check contains over 430 items in three categories that can be used to assess different facets of the partnership between the home and school. A few of the items in each of the categories are included to illustrate topics that can be surveyed to assess the correlate of positive home-school relations. Some of these items can be adapted for use in annual parent surveys that many schools conduct. If the surveys, containing the same items, are repeated year after year, the results can be analyzed to determine whether the trend in the strength of the partnership is becoming more positive or negative, or showing no change.

With regard to the issue of parents as partners and allies in student learning, ask respondents to indicate their level of agreement (strongly agree, agree, undecided, disagree, strongly disagree, or not applicable) regarding statements such as:

- Most parents understand and promote the school's mission and expectations for all students' achievement and performance.

- The school provides parents with sufficient written information regarding school rules, parent-teacher conferences, etc.
- Parent-teacher conferences focus on factors directly related to student achievement and performance on learning outcomes.

Regarding active involvement in the school, ask respondents to indicate their level of agreement (strongly agree, agree, undecided, disagree, strongly disagree, or not applicable) regarding statements such as:

- In this school, parents are involved in the formal organization, open houses, and the school program generally.
- Parents of lower-achieving students are provided extra support by the school to stimulate their participation in parent involvement activities.
- The staff involves parents in selecting, evaluating, and revising school activities.
- The school routinely solicits feedback from parents who attend school-sponsored functions and programs.

With regard to the issue of parents as teachers in the home, ask respondents to indicate their level of agreement (strongly agree, agree, undecided, disagree, strongly disagree, or not applicable) regarding statements such as:

- In this school, there is a schoolwide homework policy, and there is a consistent parent role expected.
- Parents monitor and assist their child in completing homework assignments.
- Parents and teachers work together to encourage students to do school-related work at home.

It is clear from examining this short sampling of possible survey items that, with little or no modifications, teachers could provide feedback as to how they perceive the partnership with the parents of their current students. A comparison of teacher and parent responses would offer significant insights into the parent-school relationship. Finally, secondary schools may find it interesting and valuable to ask students how they think their parents view the school and the communication and trust with the teachers.

Surveying low-income and non-English-speaking parents presents some difficulties. Getting an adequate response rate may require a home visit or a telephone call, offering the survey in another language, or having an interpreter available at school functions to help administer the survey.

Self-Report Questions

Even though many channels of communication already exist between parents and staff in their children's school, additional data may need to be collected.

For example, teachers could be asked to record the number (if any) of teacher-initiated parent-teacher conferences that were scheduled during a period of time for the purpose of discussing a discipline or academic problem. In an effort to improve positive communications, teachers might track how many teacher-initiated contacts were made to discuss student achievements and accomplishments. In addition, other indicators (such as the number of unsolicited parent phone calls to the school to express some concern) could be counted and reported out periodically. Frequent or increasing parent complaints should be considered a red flag that signals other problems and issues within the school.

Third-Party Direct Observations

Third-party observers provide an invaluable service; they gather data that would otherwise be difficult for staff members to obtain while they are engaged with students. Furthermore, as an outsider, the observer is in a position to be more objective about behaviors and situations being observed. In the area of home-school relations, an observer could observe the nature of the communications when a parent calls the school, when a parent drops by the school unexpectedly, or how the school secretary approaches calling parents on behalf of the school leader. Larry Lezotte's late friend and colleague, Wilbur Brookover, would often say that if you want to get a quick sense of a school's climate, position yourself within sight and sound of the school secretary. His notion was that the school secretary functions much like the town well in a primitive village. Every significant human interaction occurs proximate to the secretary. This example is an effective reminder that all adults in a school contribute to the overall climate of the school; however, the contributions of school secretaries, custodians, and bus drivers are often overlooked. The role they play can go a long way to elevating or depressing the learning climate of a school.

A third party could also conduct focus groups of parents and teachers to ask them their impressions of the home-school relationship, and to solicit their ideas as to how to strengthen the partnership between school and home. Focus group methodology has the advantage of being able to probe an issue in greater depth than can be done through more typical survey methodology.

Creating and maintaining a data dashboard that informs the leaders of a school about the strength of the partnership between the school and the children's homes is vital to continuous school improvement. Here again, the message should be to pick a few credible vital signs that, taken together, provide a picture of the relationship. When changes are needed, these same indicators can be used to monitor improvement over time.

Conclusion

Ron Edmonds (1974) published a paper at the Seminar on Public Policy that has direct and immediate bearing on the positive home-school relations correlate.

In this paper, Edmonds addressed the rhetorical question, "Can you get bad social service from good people?" He went on to answer this question by saying that indeed, you can get bad social service from good people. He explained that if the people to whom the social servant feels accountable are different from the clients of the service, we have the makings of bad social service, even though those who deliver the service are good people. In schools, the case is often that the typical teacher or administrator does not feel nearly as accountable to the parents of the children of the poor as they do to the middle-class parents.

Edmonds suggested that the best remedy when encountering this dichotomy of accountability toward low-income parents is to have the social servant develop a healthy respect for the clients. Educators must acknowledge that all parents are involved in their children's education, whether formally or not. They must also recognize that parents from different cultures and SES levels may be less involved because of different perceptions about education and parental roles in school or inadequate opportunities for involvement. Educators must come to recognize and value the involvement of all parents, regardless of demographics, and work to break down the barriers to parent involvement in new and creative ways.

While Edmonds's suggestion is spot-on, his advice is much easier said than done for many educators. A good place to start is by educating our teachers about challenges poor families face (Smith, 2006). In any case, the leader plays a critical role in defining the vision and the values for the school, and in creating a climate of high expectations and respect for all students and their families.

PART III

Putting the Correlates to Work in an Effective Learning System

CHAPTER 10

The Correlates in Action: A Continuous School Improvement System

The correlates of effective schools represent the knowledge educators need to successfully teach all students. By applying that knowledge, educators have the ability to create a continuous school improvement system.

Part I of this book focused on the social, political, and historical context for public education in the United States over the last century or so. With this foundation as the backdrop, we presented and discussed in part II the seven correlates of effective schools as the interdependent subsystems that must be strong and present if a school is going to ensure that the learning-for-all mission is realized.

In part III, the focus shifts from simply knowing about the effective schools concept, philosophy, and research, to actually using that knowledge as the basis for planned change in a school. In this section, we emphasize a systems approach to deploying the knowledge. Over the years, effective schools research has provided many invaluable lessons for district and school administrators, teachers, and policymakers. Based on this research and our own experience, we claim that schools and districts that heed these lessons and implement the suggested action steps with fidelity and commitment will find themselves achieving levels of success that many have thought impossible. Without question, the personal and professional satisfaction that the teachers and administrators realize when they see such success makes the journey worthwhile. After all, isn't that why we chose education as our career path?

Educational leaders at both the school and district levels need and want a continuous improvement system that has a proven performance record, one that can be implemented and maintained without significant increases in human and financial resources. In the past, many well-intentioned educational leaders tried to meet school reform expectations by simply tweaking the tactics and strategies currently used in the schools. While this piecemeal approach has produced some improvements in assessed student learning, most would agree that such efforts have fallen short of what was wanted and needed.

During the last several years, much of the change that schools struggled to implement, though well intentioned, may be described as school leaders metaphorically picking the "low-hanging fruit." At this point in the journey, most of the low-hanging fruit has been harvested and now it's time for the educational leaders to find and use strategies that will allow them to harvest the fruit that's higher up in the educational tree. This new and higher reach means that the change efforts are going to challenge beliefs and values, and policies and practices that have been held sacred for a long time.

Creating the Context for the Effective Learning System

Imagine that educational leaders wrote a want ad to be published in various professional journals and newspapers for the purpose of describing their need for a proven process to guide their schools and districts to the deeper changes needed. What would they put in the ad? The current reform environment demands that schools and districts secure a system that is responsive to the six dimensions, all of which are integral to the correlates of effective schools:

1. **Results-oriented**—The standards and accountability movement, a prominent focus in education policy since 2000, has changed the game when it comes to defining what evidence will be used to judge the effectiveness of the school or district. This focus represents a deep cultural change from the past. Previously, the various accreditation models centered their evaluation on the inputs and processes in the school, not the outputs. From what we have observed, there seems to be little indication that parents, political leaders, and business leaders have any desire to back away from results as the accepted currency or bottom line for judging school effectiveness. It is safe to assume that there will be many heated discussions among these educational stakeholders regarding what results should be used to monitor a school's effectiveness. In all likelihood, the effectiveness of schools and teachers will continue to be judged by student performance.

2. **Research-based**—Historically, individual and small groups of educators decided what programs and practices would operate within a school or district. The programs and practices did not change as long as the local champions for those decisions remained in place. Unfortunately, this cultural practice has two significant problems associated with it. First, the champion's advocacy may or may not be based on research or best practices. Often a practice is embraced simply on the basis of a teacher's (or the champion's) belief that it will work on behalf of the school's learning goals. Second,

even if the strategy, practice, or program is found to be effective in advancing goals, it will likely be abandoned if the champion leaves the school. The new reality for decision-making in selecting new programs, practices, and strategies requires the would-be champions to incorporate research findings into their advocacy. Teacher commitment to a program, practice, or strategy is a necessary (but not sufficient) condition for success. The best solution is to incorporate teacher enthusiasm with proven research findings. Similarly, when the local champion moves on, student achievement results should be used to decide whether to retain, modify, or abandon a practice.

3. **Data-driven**—Historically, supporters of public education were much more likely to accept professional judgment as the accepted standard of proof. For example, the majority of today's senior citizens grew up in a time when one did not question the physician. Similarly, the teacher's judgment was rarely questioned when it came to comments about the students. Times have changed. The new reality is that parents, patients, citizens, and would-be customers routinely demand, "Show me the data!" The demand to see the supporting data should not be misconstrued to mean that professional judgment is always wrong and that professionals can't be trusted. The new reality seems to be based on two assumptions. First, the standard of proof needed to be raised across the board because there were too many incidents where the judgments proved to be erroneous, especially when it came to the educability of the children of poverty. Second, if the professional's judgment is correct, credible data should support it, making the judgment even more convincing. Educational leaders have to implement and maintain a data management system that can provide credible evidence of the system's functioning, whether one is talking about the progress of an individual student or the performance of the entire system. The number of possible indicators that could be used to measure and monitor the system's performance is virtually unlimited. School leaders need a data-driven system where the indicators that are measured and monitored over time are few in number, valid for the intended purpose, and credible to the users.

4. **Focused on both quality and equity**—The level of achievement that students attain has always been of interest to parents and politicians concerned about education. Traditionally, some measure of central tendency (average or median achievement) was the standard of evidence used to communicate level of achievement. The new reality for educational leaders requires them to consider the variability around that measure of central tendency. Concerned stakeholders want to know how various student groups (minority, disadvantaged, and special needs, for example) are performing on the indicators of interest. This need has given birth to wide use of the concept of data disaggregation. Most contemporary educators have become familiar with the process of disaggregating student performance data. Consequently, they are beginning to demand that producers of curriculum and instructional materials provide disaggregated data on the program's impact on different

subgroups of students. With this data, educators are able to make more informed decisions about which instructional resources will best serve the students in the school or district. Likewise, parents have come to expect that annual reports of a school's progress or performance will be presented and discussed so that everyone can see who is profiting how much for the school's efforts.

5. **Collaborative in form**—David Tyack and Lawrence Cuban, in their book *Tinkering Toward Utopia* (1997), noted that most efforts to reform schools during the 1900s were advocated by what they called the "outside evangelists" for reform. They went on to say that most efforts to change schools by these outside evangelists died on the front steps of the school. The authors concluded that significant and sustainable reform is virtually impossible unless or until those who make up the professional community of the school are committed to the proposed reforms. The new reality for school leaders reveals the pendulum swing from the outside-in change strategy to the inside-out change strategy. The advocates of the new strategy have concluded that the best hope for true and long-term school reform must be led by the men and women on the firing line of the school, namely the teachers and school level administrators. The most popular trend sweeping the educational landscape is the concept of schools as professional learning communities (PLCs). Its popularity derives, in part, from the focus on activities that are teacher-centered, embedded in practice, and collaborative. The PLC concept, when implemented correctly, ensures that the school staff will be engaged in meaningful dialogue that will create valid and sustainable reform strategies. Given this new reality, most school leaders agree that a model or process is needed to guide reform centered on collaboration among the stakeholders. As important as anything, a model can provide the diverse groups within a school with a common language that makes it easier for professional conversation to occur. Collaborative groups will always face a challenge finding enough time to meet and talk. Therefore, to make the best use of the scarce resource of time, a shared language is essential.

6. **Ongoing and self-renewing**—The focus on school reform has led to changes in accreditation processes for schools. In the past, schools submitted documents to the regional accreditation agency every five years (and in some cases, more or less frequently). These processes began to change when, in the United States, the individual state agencies began to require the schools to develop annual plans for school improvement. For several years, schools labored to meet this new mandate. Now they are facing what might be called the final frontier in school improvement. Today, schools and districts must develop and implement systems to support continuous improvement and provide evidence of progress. Continuous improvement, by definition, requires constant monitoring of the vital signs regarding the health of the school and its interdependent subsystems. However, constant monitoring must be coupled with a

willingness to adjust current policies, practices, and procedures when the vital signs demand it. The two core beliefs that constitute the foundation for continuous school improvement are (1) continuous improvement can start anytime, and (2) there is no end to continuous improvement. There will always be a next level to which the school, district, or any other organization aspires.

Continuous School Improvement Based on Effective Schools Research

Effective schools research and associated proven practices constitute an especially valid framework for satisfying school leaders' needs as they respond to the new realities of school reform. The effective schools framework is based on several beliefs and assumptions that can be easily aligned with the six new realities of school reform described in the previous section. These factors are central to achieving school improvement through implementation of the correlates:

1. All children can learn and come to school motivated to do so.

2. The individual school controls enough of the variables to ensure that all students learn.

3. The school's immediate stakeholders (administrators and teachers) are the most qualified and best-positioned to implement the needed changes.

4. The current teachers and administrators are already doing the best they know to do, given the conditions in which they find themselves.

5. School-by-school change is the best hope for reforming the schools.

6. For the foreseeable future, schools will be expected to focus on learning for all as their primary mission.

7. Schools will be held accountable for measurable performance results; technology accelerators will be used to increase the rate of feedback in instructional monitoring systems.

8. Educational equity will receive even greater emphasis as the number of poor and minority students continues to increase (as a proportion of the total school-age population).

9. School empowerment and staff collaboration will emphasize the utilization of research and proven practices for planning school change.

10. School leaders will be expected to demonstrate skills both as efficient managers and effective visionary leaders.

The Continuous Improvement System

Figure 10.1 (page 136) introduces the seven process components that schools and districts must address if they are going to successfully use this framework and benefit from the many years of research and case studies of effective schools. The graphic has two interdependent dimensions. The dimension on the left describes conceptual and content-related components (establish the process; clarify the mission, core values, and core beliefs; and identify essential student learnings). These three components, while not cut in stone, are relatively more static than the other four components shown on the right side of the graphic. The cyclical feature on the right defines the actions for the improvement process (study, reflect, plan, and do). While each of these actions is vital to the success of the process, each step can and should be customized to suit the needs of the individual school.

In previous publications, we have described this framework in detail: *Assembly Required: A Continuous School Improvement System* (Lezotte & McKee, 2002), and *Stepping Up: Leading the Charge to Improve Our Schools* (Lezotte & McKee, 2006). In the remainder of this chapter, we briefly describe each of the seven components in this framework for continuous improvement. We highlight where the correlates presented in the earlier chapters fit together and form a coherent process that will enable committed educators to continuously improve their schools.

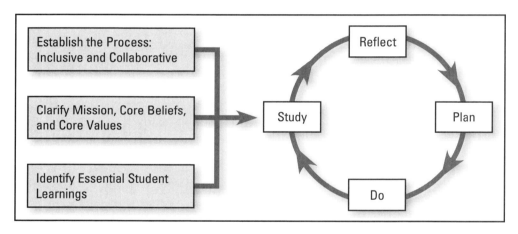

Figure 10.1: The continuous school improvement process.

Establish the Process

The effective schools framework for continuous improvement is based on broad involvement of staff and other stakeholders in an ongoing process. One approach that has served many successful schools well is to identify a school leadership team made up of a cross-section of teachers and other support staff in the school. In addition, the school leadership team should involve more stakeholders by creating a professional learning team for each correlate. Depending on the size of the school faculty, each correlate team should have anywhere from four to nine members.

The expectations for each correlate team are to:

1. Become the smartest group in the school about research and best practices related to their assigned correlate.

2. Design and implement the data dashboard for monitoring the correlate in their school.

3. Make recommendations for change in the school relative to the correlate.

The creation of correlate teams serves many purposes; one of the most important is to involve more staff in the process, thus broadening the base of involvement and increasing the commitment to the adopted change strategies. While there is no guarantee that involvement will lead to commitment, the odds are good that those who have been given voice in the process will buy into it. In this step, the correlate of instructional leadership takes the stage. It is up to the school leaders, especially the principal, to establish a climate of trust and inclusiveness. This is where the courageous leader lets go of the top-down, authoritarian vision of leadership and embraces distributive leadership, empowering staff members to take leadership roles appropriate to their skills. Schools wishing to improve their relationship with parents and the community can also involve parents and the community on correlate teams as appropriate, in keeping with the correlate of positive home-school relations.

Clarify the Mission, Beliefs, and Values

Unlike people in many other organizations, educators seem to be willing to accept unquestioned assumptions that all the adults that work in a school have the same or at least very similar beliefs and values relative to the purpose of education, the nature of learning, and the role of the teacher. In reality, teachers have different mindsets about these and other important issues. The goal of more effective organizations, including schools, is to make sure that all the people subscribe to the same values, priorities, and sense of mission.

Popular motivational speaker and author Dennis Waitley (1993) stated that organizations, like people, are always moving in the direction of their dominant thoughts. Clarifying the mission, beliefs, and values represents an attempt to create a laser-like focus on the energy in the organization. When the culture of a school reflects an intentional and coherent set of beliefs and values, the school is much more likely to be successful in realizing its mission.

At this step of the process, the correlates of clear and focused mission, high expectations for success, and instructional leadership emerge—and merge—front and center. School leaders must strive to clearly communicate the vision and the mission, the moral imperative behind the vision, and inspire stakeholders to action in pursuit of the mission. Several process steps can be used to help bring the desired clarity and focus to the participants in the improvement activities. A good test of the effort to clarify and focus the beliefs, values, and mission is to randomly ask stakeholders this question, "What does this school care most about?" The answers stakeholders provide should be virtually the same or very similar. Anything short of a high degree of consensus should be interpreted to mean that there is still more work to be done.

Identify Essential Student Learnings

The standards and accountability movement has mandated grade-by-grade, subject-by-subject standards for most schools. These standards documents are intended to convey what various states or provinces want their student-citizens to know and be able to do as they move through and graduate from school.

At one level, these standards could be interpreted as the student's essential learnings. Unfortunately, identifying the actual essential learnings is not that simple. Notably, states and provinces have tended to mandate more standards for a given grade or subject than can be reasonably taught to a mastery level in the time available. Furthermore, some of the most important outcomes of education are almost never found in these standards statements.

This step in the process is designed to make clear what must be taught and learned and what may be set aside if time is not available to teach all the standards to the expected level of mastery. For many educators, the challenge of this step is coming to accept the reality that some things matter more than others in both the short and long term. With time to teach being one of the most precious and scarcest resources available to schools, some difficult choices must be made.

The deliverables coming out of these difficult deliberations are what this process calls the essential student learnings. The vertical alignment of the school as a hierarchical system demands that teachers prepare their students for the next level of instruction. The sequential nature of this process should prompt educators to begin at the top with what graduates should know and be able to do, and work backward to identify what students need to know to meet those requirements. This backward mapping process continues on down the line until every grade has clear standards regarding what should be learned before a student is sent on to the next level. It is then up to the teachers to ensure that students learn what they need to know to be successful at that next level of schooling.

Clearly, opportunity to learn/time on task is the correlate most closely related to this step in the process. The high expectations for success correlate also plays a role as the staff determines what students should know and be able to do as a result of schooling. Like mission, beliefs, and values, and the involvement process itself, the essential student learnings, once identified, will be relatively stable from year to year. They should, however, be reviewed from time to time and modified as standards change.

Now we turn to the dynamic part of the continuous improvement framework and process. This examination makes it immediately clear why the first three components need to be in place before meaningful improvement actions can be taken.

Study the Data

The first question to ask as we begin the dynamic phase of continuous school improvement is, "How is the school doing?" The school leaders who have been called upon to answer the question may rightly ask, "How is the school doing relative to what?" The answer is relative to mission, beliefs, values, and essential student learnings that the school leadership and stakeholders have defined. Clearly, school leaders cannot answer the question unless they have completed the first three steps.

Examining the data associated with student mastery of the essential learnings using the process of disaggregation represents a problem-finding strategy. Virtually all problem-solving models begin with a description of the problem to be solved. Disaggregating student performance data to assess progress on essential learnings provides the needed focus for the problem. It is important to recognize that disaggregating student performance data is not a problem-solving strategy. These analyses do not inform what change strategies should be adopted; however, they can pinpoint what problems should be addressed.

In order for the school leadership team to identify potential change strategies, they need to undertake a process of root cause analysis. As we said at the outset of this book, the correlates of effective schools represent an important set of the leading indicators of learning in school. That is to say that when the seven correlates are proven to be present and strong in a school, student learning will improve and the school's mission will come to fruition. Therefore, once the problems have been framed, each correlate team should be asked to drill down on the correlate data to determine whether change on that correlate is needed. For example, if the data associated with the correlate of safe and orderly environment indicates that the disciplinary climate is not conducive to learning, improvement is needed.

Not every problem in the school requires change on all seven correlates. The correlate teams should incorporate their experience and expertise and the associated research to make informed judgments on what to change. Likewise, the leadership team can ask each correlate team to provide input and recommendations if they determine that one or more of the school's core beliefs or values need attention.

Conducting root cause analyses is an invaluable tool that allows schools to more precisely define the specific causes of problems. Like disaggregation, root cause analysis does not provide a solution to the problems. This process serves to narrow the change dialogue. Otherwise, the school leadership team may try to solve a problem that is so general that the intended improvement may not be realized.

Reflect

The work conducted in the study phase of the continuous improvement process identifies problems that need to be addressed in pursuit of the mission. The work to be completed in the reflect phase of the process is to search and find solutions to the identified problems. Stated improvement goals are the deliverables from this phase.

In this step, the leadership and the individual correlate teams engage in internal and external scanning for solutions. Using internal scanning strategies, correlate teams look to colleagues for suggestions, ideas, or proven practices. The external scanning strategies require the teams to look outside the school for possible strategies. Some of the scanning strategies include looking at published research and proven practices, attending professional conferences, and visiting schools that have successfully addressed similar problems.

Generally, our experience suggests that it is better for a school to have only a few improvement goals (two or three). Multiple action plans can be developed for each improvement goal.

Plan

At this point in the process, the problems have been identified and the improvement goals have been determined. Now the process involves deciding what to do with the collected information: develop an implementation plan.

An improvement goal aimed at improving student reading performance may have one action plan for each of three or four of the correlates. For example, to improve reading performance, the school may plan to increase parent involvement, increase time on task, improve the disciplinary climate of the school, and raise teacher expectations.

For the most part, staff members must implement the change strategies even while they are fully engaged in the day-to-day operations of the school. The leadership team needs to create a realistic timetable for implementing the multiple action plans and improvement goals. Many school leadership teams have used Gantt charts. It lays out the tasks to be completed and the timetable for their completion. These easy-to-follow charts indicate what tasks will be completed by whom and when.

The Gantt chart process makes it possible for the leadership team to sequence events in such a way that staff can complete the tasks without becoming overwhelmed. Each action plan would constitute a Gantt chart. So, if the school leadership team had agreed to three improvement goals and each goal had two action plans, a total of six improvement Gantt charts would constitute the entire school plan.

Our past experience suggests that the school leadership team should also develop Gantt charts to evaluate progress. The program- or project-evaluation Gantt charts stipulate what data will be collected when, and by whom, throughout the implementation process. These data will be used to determine whether the action plan was successfully implemented and achieved its intended purpose. Conducting quality program evaluations is relatively easy if the evaluation plan is developed before the action steps are implemented. It is much more difficult to go back after the fact and reconstruct the story.

Do

All the work that has to be invested in this or any other continuous improvement process will not result in positive change unless the intended action steps are implemented with quality and commitment. The oversight responsibility of the school leadership team is especially critical for successful school reform.

Schools are extremely complex and busy places. It is very easy for change activities to get lost in the buzz of day-to-day school life. To be successful, change efforts need champions. The school leadership team and the individual correlate teams must accept responsibility to act as the champions for their change strategies.

The logic of continuous improvement means that once the action plans have been implemented and evaluated, the dynamic cycle repeats itself. Now the leadership and correlate teams repeat the question, "How are we doing?" This may lead to three possible conclusions. First, the evaluation data suggest that the problem has been solved. Second, the problem has not been solved and more—or different—work is needed. Third, the problem has been positively impacted, but needs more effort.

The long-term aim of the continuous improvement process is to create a cultural mindset among staff whereby these actions define "how we do things around here." Once this is accomplished, when the champions move on—and they will—those left behind will pick up the banner of continuous school improvement and keep the momentum going. Clearly, the process described here reflects the six dimensions that schools and districts are seeking. The process, when executed with fidelity and commitment, is data-driven, research-based, results-oriented, focused on quality and equity, collaborative in form, and ongoing and self-renewing. The history of continuous school improvement based on the effective schools framework that has been published in numerous books attests to its success in advancing the learning-for-all mission.

School Effectiveness and Teacher Effectiveness

Throughout our discussion of the correlates of effective schools and the continuous school improvement process, we have not specifically addressed teacher effectiveness. This omission should not be interpreted to suggest that the quality of teaching and the vital role that teachers play is unimportant. We left this topic out for two reasons. First, our goal in writing this book is to address the issue of the school as a complex system, a demanding undertaking in and of itself. Second, we assert that before the quality of teaching can be addressed in a straightforward way, evidence must show that the school as a system is actually designed to achieve its intended aim—learning for all.

Professor Madeline Hunter, in conversation with Larry Lezotte, was asked how she saw the relationship between school effectiveness and teacher effectiveness. She responded by stating that she thought that effective schools research and the correlates represented an organizational umbrella under which effective teaching could and would flourish. A corollary of Professor Hunter's apt description would be that the effective schools organizational umbrella would also make it possible for ineffective teaching to stand out and be addressed.

Some leaders at both school and district levels have reinterpreted the correlates of effective schools down to the classroom level. They have found the translation easy and useful. For example, classrooms, like the schools in which they reside, must be characterized by a safe and orderly environment, a clear and focused mission, and have a teacher with high expectations in charge (one who acts as the instructional leader of the students).

This discussion leaves us with a final question. What percentage of the teacher workforce in a school, district, or even an entire state, province, or country would be judged effective if schools were truly designed to support the mission of learning for all? The potential for success would be unlimited. Conversely, if educators fail to embrace the correlates of effective schools and adopt a practical and inclusive process to implement them, it seems unlikely that even with a staff of effective teachers, the learning-for-all mission will be fully achieved.

A Final Thought Addressed to School Leaders

We've all heard the expression "Begin with the end in mind, design down, and deliver up." This entire book (and for that matter the entire effective schools movement that began in the late 1960s) has had a single end in mind—learning for all. The accumulation of the numerous research studies that now define the knowledge base for the effective schools movement provide the "design down" blueprint for schools committed to the learning-for-all mission. Published case studies of schools and districts that have implemented and sustained school improvement based on the research illustrate the "deliver up" aspect of the expression. It is clear that the essential components for making more schools more effective are known and readily available. Unfortunately, regardless of the number of research studies that validate the effective schools concept, regardless of the number of published case studies of successful schools and districts, there is a single ingredient that can't be provided from outside the school. That ingredient is personal commitment to the mission and the tasks involved in building and sustaining it. The leaders or leadership groups must decide that they are going to make an unwavering commitment to the mission of learning for all.

The decision to commit is not dependent upon having the knowledge and skills required—knowledge and skills can be learned. This decision is not an intellectual argument that leaders must have with themselves—educational leaders know that it is the right thing to do. The decision to make the unwavering commitment to the learning-for-all mission starts in the heart of every educational leader. Continuous school improvement based on the effective schools research and attendant practices is not a technical adjustment in the ways of the school, and it is not an intellectual calculation; rather, it is a moral journey, first and foremost.

We end this book with a story about two stonecutters engaged in their trade. When the first stonecutter was asked what he was doing he said, "Cutting stone." When the second stonecutter was asked what he was doing, he said, "Building a cathedral." As a school leader, are you the stonecutter or the cathedral builder?

APPENDIX A

Suggested Foundational Research Readings on the Correlates of Effective Schools

Many individuals were involved in the early research that helped establish the correlates of effective schools, many of whom have been referenced earlier in this text. While it would be impossible to cite them all within the confines of these pages, we have listed a few more for those who are interested in the early research.

Anderson, L. W. (1983). Policy implications of research on school time. *School Administrator, 40*(11), 25–28.

Austin, G. R. (1979). Exemplary schools and the search for effectiveness. *Educational Leadership, 37*(1), 10–14.

Averich, H. A., Carroll, S. J., Donaldson, T. S., Kiesling, H. J., & Pincus, J. (1972). *How effective is schooling? A critical review and synthesis of research findings.* Santa Monica, CA: RAND.

Brookover, W. B., & Schneider, J. M. (1975). Academic environments and elementary school achievement. *Journal of Research and Development in Education, 9*(1), 82–91.

Brookover, W. B., Schweitzer, J. H., Schneider, J. M., Beady, C. H., Flood, P. K., & Wisenbaker, J. M. (1978). Elementary school social climate and school achievement. *American Educational Research Journal, 15*(2), 301–318.

Clark, D., Lotto, L., & McCarthy, M. (1980). Factors associated with success in urban elementary schools. *Phi Delta Kappan, 61*(7), 467–470.

Edmonds, R. (1979). *Search for effective schools: The identification and analysis of city schools that are instructionally effective for poor children.* Washington, DC: National Institute of Education. (ERIC Document Reproduction Service No. ED142610)

Eubanks, E. E., & Levine, D. U. (1983). A first look at effective schools projects in New York City and Milwaukee. *Phi Delta Kappan, 64*(10), 697–702.

Klitgaard, R. E., & Hall, G. R. (1973). *A statistical search for unusually effective schools.* Santa Monica, CA: RAND. (ERIC Document Reproduction Service No. ED085409)

Levine, D. (1982). Successful approaches for improving academic achievement in inner-city elementary schools. *Phi Delta Kappan, 63*(8), 523–526.

Murphy, J. F., Weil, M., Hallinger, P., & Mitman, A. (1982). Academic press: Translating high expectations into school policies and classroom practices. *Educational Leadership, 40*(3), 22–26.

Office of Program Evaluation and Research, California Department of Education. (1977). *California school effectiveness study: The first year: 1974–1975.* Sacramento, CA: Author.

Phi Delta Kappa. (1980). *Why do some urban schools succeed?* Bloomington, IN: Author.

Purkey, S., & Smith, M. (1983). Effective schools—A review. *Elementary School Journal, 83*(4), 427–452.

Slavin, R. E. (1980). Effects of individual learning expectations on student achievement. *Journal of Educational Psychology, 72*(4), 520–524.

Sweeney, J. (1982). Research synthesis on effective school leadership. *Educational Leadership, 39*(5), 346–352.

Venezky, R. L., & Winfield, L. F. (1979). *Schools that succeed beyond expectations in teaching: Studies in education* (Tech. Rep. No. 1). Newark: University of Delaware. (ERIC Document Reproduction Service ED177484)

Effective Schools Online Tools

Because we reference these tools throughout the book, we thought it'd be appropriate to describe them in detail here.

Reality Check

Reality Check is an online surveying tool offered by Effective Schools Products. Reality Check contains a database of over 1,800 survey questions specifically designed around the correlates of effective schools. Users can modify any of the questions, as well as create completely new ones, so each survey can be tailored to a school or district's specific needs. Surveys can be created in English or Spanish, and can be conducted online or in paper-and-pencil format. Online responses are tabulated as they are received, and responses from hard copy surveys can be easily entered. Data are automatically tabulated and users can disaggregate the data in a variety of ways. If a school or district conducts the same survey for two or more years, Reality Check enables the user to do a trend analysis—a very useful feature for determining progress on the correlates.

This tool is an economical and efficient way to solicit perceptual data from your stakeholders. For more information on Reality Check, visit www.effectiveschools .com.

Effective Schools Research LiNK

The Research LiNK is a comprehensive online resource of school improvement research offered by Effective Schools Products. This extensive, searchable database contains more than 1,600 research summaries on topics ranging from classroom strategies to what works at the district level and everything in between. Another seventy-two summaries are added each year, keeping the LiNK relevant and updated.

Professional educators translate the research into everyday language so you can understand the study without wading through pages of statistics and jargon. The writers summarize the key findings and implications of each study so that you can quickly determine if it's relevant to your needs. The LiNK is organized around the correlates of effective schools, making it very easy to use. You can search by topic, title, author, or keyword, and then simply print what you need without retyping or reformatting.

For more information on Research LiNK, visit www.effectiveschools.com.

References and Resources

Alexander, K. L., Entwisle, D. R., & Olson, L. S. (2007). Lasting consequences of the summer learning gap. *American Sociological Review, 72*(2), 167–180.

Allen, L. (2001). From plaques to practice: How schools can breathe life into their guiding beliefs. *Phi Delta Kappan, 83*(4), 289–293.

Amatea, E. S., & Vandiver, F. (2004). Best practices: Expanding the school leadership team—using counselors to facilitate teacher collaboration with families. *Journal of School Leadership, 14*(3), 327–344.

Anderson, G., & Davenport, P. (2002). *Closing the achievement gap—no excuses.* Houston, TX: American Productivity and Quality Center.

Astor, R. A., Meyer, H. A., & Behre, W. J. (1999). Unknown places and times: Maps and interviews about violence in high schools. *American Educational Research Journal, 36*(1), 3–42.

Axelrod, R. (2002). *Terms of engagement: Changing the way we change organizations.* San Francisco: Berrett-Koehler.

Baccellieri, P. (2010). *Professional learning communities: Using data in decision making to improve student learning.* Huntington, CA: Shell Education.

Barber, M., & Mourshed, M. (2007). *How the world's best-performing school systems come out on top.* London: McKinsey and Company.

Barton, P. E. (2005). *One third of a nation: Rising dropout rates and declining opportunities.* Princeton, NJ: Policy Information Center, Educational Testing Service.

Bennis, W. (1989). *Why leaders can't lead: The unconscious conspiracy continues.* San Francisco: Jossey-Bass.

Berkey, T., & Dow, E. (2008). Texas school beats the odds with a shared commitment to student learning. *Journal of Staff Development, 29*(4), 31–34.

Blankstein, A. M., Houston, P. D., & Cole, R. W. (Eds.). (2009). *Building sustainable leadership capacity.* Thousand Oaks, CA: Corwin Press.

Bodovski, K., & Farkas, G. (2007). Mathematics growth in early elementary school: The roles of beginning knowledge, student engagement, and instruction. *Elementary School Journal, 108*(2), 115–130.

Booher-Jennings, J. (2005). Below the bubble: Educational triage and the Texas accountability system. *American Educational Research Journal, 42*(2), 231–268.

Borman, G. D., & Dowling, N. M. (2006). Longitudinal achievement effects of multiyear summer school: Evidence from the teach Baltimore randomized field test. *Educational Evaluation and Policy Analysis, 28*(1), 25–48.

Bossidy, L., & Charan, R. (2002). *Execution: The discipline of getting things done.* New York: Crown Business.

Bowsher, J. E. (2003). *Successful administrators leading successful schools.* San Diego: Jack E. Bowsher.

Branson, R. K. (1987). Why the schools can't improve: The upper-limit hypothesis. *Journal of Instructional Development, 10*(4), 5–26.

Branson, R. K. (2000). *Alternative models of schooling: Technology defeats obsolescence.* Accessed at www.cpt.fsu.edu/pdf/alternativemodels.pdf on August 5, 2009.

Briggs, K. L., & Wohlstetter, P. (2003). Key elements of a successful school-based management strategy. *School Effectiveness and School Improvement, 14*(3), 351–372.

Brookover, W. B., & Lezotte, L. W. (1977). *Changes in school characteristics coincident with changes in student achievement.* East Lansing: Michigan State University, College of Urban Development.

Brown, K. M., & Anfara, V. A., Jr. (2002). The walls of division crumble as ears, mouths, minds and hearts open: A unified profession of middle-level administrators and teachers. *International Journal of Leadership in Education, 5*(1), 33–49.

Brown, L. (2004). Project succeed academy: A public-private partnership to develop a holistic approach for serving students with behavior problems. *Urban Education, 39*(1), 5–32.

Carroll, J. B. (1963). A model for school learning. *Teachers College Record, 64*(8), 723–733.

Cawelti, G. (Ed.). (1999). *Handbook of research on improving student achievement* (2nd ed.). Arlington, VA: Educational Research Service.

Cawelti, G., & Protheroe, N. (2001). *High student achievement: How six school districts changed into high-performance systems.* Arlington, VA: Educational Research Service.

Chenoweth, K. (2007). *It's being done.* Cambridge, MA: Harvard Education Press.

Chhuon, V., Gilkey, E., Gonzalez, M., Daly, A., & Chrispeels, J. (2008). The little district that could: The process of building district-school trust. *Educational Administration Quarterly, 44*(2), 227–281.

Cohen, M. T. (1993). Changing schools from within. *Journal of School Leadership, 3*(3), 269–287.

Coleman, J. S. (1966). *Equality of educational opportunity.* Washington, DC: U.S. Government Printing Office.

Collins, J. (2002). *Good to great: Why companies make the leap . . . and others don't.* New York: HarperCollins.

Comer, J. P. (1998). Educating poor minority children. *Scientific American, 259*(5), 42–48.

Conyers, L. M., Reynolds, A. J., & Ou, S. R. (2003). The effect of early childhood intervention and subsequent special education services: Findings from the Chicago child-parent centers. *Educational Evaluation and Policy Analysis, 25*(1), 75–95.

Cooper, H., Nye, B., Charlton, K., Lindsay, J., & Greathouse, S. (1996). The effects of summer vacation on achievement test scores: A narrative and meta-analytic review. *Review of Educational Research, 66*, 227–268.

Cotton, K. (2000). *The schooling practices that matter most.* Portland, OR: Northwest Regional Education Laboratory; Alexandria, VA: Association for Supervision and Curriculum Development.

Covey, S. R. (1989). *Seven habits of highly effective people.* New York: Simon & Schuster.

Creighton, T. B. (2001). Data analysis and the principalship. *Principal Leadership: High School Edition, 1*(9), 52–57.

Cremin, L. A. (1976). *Public education.* New York: Basic Books.

Currie, J. (2005). *Health disparities and gaps in school readiness: Closing racial and ethnic gaps.* Accessed at www.princeton.edu/futureofchildren/publications/journals/article/index.xml?journalid=38&articleid=119 on September 12, 2009.

Darling-Hammond, L. (1995). Restructuring schools for student success. *Daedalus, 124,* 53–162.

Darling-Hammond, L., & McCloskey, L. (2008). Assessment for learning around the world: What would it mean to be internationally competitive. *Phi Delta Kappan, 90*(4), 263–272.

Darling-Hammond, L., & Rustique-Forrester, E. (2005). The consequences of student testing for teaching and teacher quality. In J. L. Herman & E. H. Haertel (Eds.), *Uses and misuses of data for educational accountability and improvement* (pp. 289–319). Malden, MA: Blackwell.

Deal, T. E., & Peterson, K. D. (1999). *Shaping school culture: The heart of leadership.* San Francisco: Jossey-Bass.

Deming, W. E. (1993). *The new economics: For industry, government, education.* Cambridge, MA: Massachusetts Institute of Technology.

Denton, D. R. (2002). *Summer school: Unfulfilled promise.* Atlanta, GA: Southern Regional Education Board.

Donelson, W. J., & Donelson, R. W. (2010). *Implementing response to intervention.* Huntington Beach, CA: Shell Education.

Donovan, M. S., & Bransford, J. D. (Eds.). (2005). *How students learn: History, mathematics, and science in the classroom.* Washington: National Academies Press.

DuFour, R., & Eaker, R. (1998). *Professional learning communities at work™: Best practices for enhancing student achievement.* Bloomington, IN: Solution Tree Press (formerly National Educational Service).

Duke, N. K. (2000). For the rich it's richer: Print experiences and environments offered to children in very low- and very high-socioeconomic status first-grade classrooms. *American Educational Research Journal, 37*(2), 441–478.

Duran, R. P. (2002). Technology, education, and at-risk students. *Educating at-risk students.* Chicago: National Society for the Study of Education.

Dweck, C. (2006). *Mindset: The new psychology of success.* New York: Random House.

Edmonds, R. (1974). *Minimums and maximums: A theory and design of social service reform.* Accessed at www.eric.ed.gov/ERICWebPortal/custom/portlets/recordDetails/detailmini.jsp?_nfpb=true&_&ERICExtSearch_SearchValue_0=ED106387&ERICExtSearch_SearchType_0=no&accno=ED106387 on May 17, 2010. (ERIC Document Reproduction Service No. ED106387)

Edmonds, R. (1979). Effective schools for the urban poor. *Educational Leadership, 37*(3), 15–18, 20–24.

Edmonds, R. (1982). Programs of school improvement: An overview. *Educational Leadership, 40*(3), 8–11.

Edmonds, R., & Frederiksen, J. R. (1978). *Search for effective schools: The identification and analysis of city schools that are instructionally effective for poor children.* Cambridge, MA: Harvard University Center for Urban Studies.

Entwisle, D. R., & Alexander, K. L. (1992). Summer setback: Race, poverty, school composition, and mathematics achievement in the first two years of school. *American Sociological Review, 57*(1), 72–84.

Epstein, J. L., & Hollifield, J. H. (1996). Title I and school-family-community partnerships: Using research to realize the potential. *Journal of Education for Students Placed at Risk, 3,* 263–278.

Epstein, J. L., Sanders, M. G., Simon, B. S., Salinas, K. C., Jansorn, N. R., & Van Voorhis, F. L. (2002). *School, family, and community partnerships: Your handbook for action* (2nd ed.). Thousand Oaks, CA: Corwin Press.

Fielding, L., Kerr, N., & Rosier, P. (2007). *Annual growth for all students, catch-up growth for those who are behind.* Kennewick, WA: New Foundation Press.

Finnan, C., Schnepel, K. C., & Anderson, L. W. (2003). Powerful learning environment: The critical link between school and classroom cultures. *Journal for Education for Students Placed at Risk, 8*(4), 391–418.

Fisher, D., Grant, M., Frey, N., & Johnson, C. (2007/2008). Taking formative assessment schoolwide. *Educational Leadership, 65*(4), 65–68.

Florida Virtual School. (2009). *Florida virtual school.* Accessed at www.flvs.net on July 10, 2009.

Fredericksen, J. (1975). *School effectiveness and equality of educational opportunity.* Cambridge, MA: Harvard University, Center for Urban Studies.

Fullan, M. (2002). The change leader. *Educational Leadership, 59*(8), 16–21.

Gaddy, G. D. (1988). High school order and academic achievement. *American Journal of Education, 96*(4), 496–518.

Gagné, R. M. (1985). *The conditions of learning and theory of instruction* (4th ed.). New York: Holt, Rinehart and Winston.

Garrity, D. T., & Burris, C. C. (2007). Personalized learning in detracked classrooms. *School Administrator, 64*(8), 10–16.

Giles, C., Johnson, L., Brooks, S., & Jacobson, S. L. (2005). Building bridges, building community: Transformational leadership in a challenging urban context. *Journal of School Leadership, 25*(5), 519–545.

Gladwell, M. (2008). *Outliers: The story of success.* Boston: Little, Brown and Company.

Goddard, R. D., Hoy, W. K., & Hoy, A. W. (2000). Collective teacher efficacy: Its meaning, measure, and impact on student achievement. *American Educational Research Journal, 37*(2), 479–507.

Goddard, R. D., Hoy, W. K., & Hoy, A. W. (2004). Collective efficacy beliefs: Theoretical developments, empirical evidence, and future directions. *Educational Researcher, 33*(3), 3–13.

Goddard, R. D., Logerfo, L., & Hoy, W. K. (2004). High school accountability: The role of perceived collective efficacy. *Educational Policy, 18*(3), 403–425.

Good, T. L. (1987). Teacher expectations and student perceptions: A decade of research. *Educational Leadership, 44*(5), 415–422.

Good, T. L., & Brophy, J. E. (1991). *Looking in classrooms* (5th ed.). New York: HarperCollins.

Goodman, C. C. (2006). Let's do lunch together. *Principal Leadership, 7*(4), 31–35.

Green, D. G. (2006). Welcome to the house system. *Educational Leadership, 63*(7), 64–67.

Grossman, J., Campbell, M., & Raley, B. (2007). *Quality time after school: What instructors can do to enhance learning.* Philadelphia: Public/Private Ventures.

Guskey, T. R., & Passaro, P. D. (1994). Teacher efficacy: A study of construct dimensions. *American Educational Research Journal, 31*, 627–643.

Halverson, R., Grigg, J., Prichett, R., & Thomas, C. (2007). The new instructional leadership: Creating data-driven instructional systems in school. *Journal of School Leadership, 17*(2), 159–193.

Hammond, J. (1995). Managing for high performance: A superintendent's nine rules for a results-oriented school system. *School Administrator, 10*, 12–16.

Hassrick, E. M., & Schneider, B. (2009). Parent surveillance in schools: A question of social class. *American Journal of Education, 115*, 195–225.

Hattie, J., & Timperley, H. (2007). The power of feedback. *Review of Educational Research, 77*(1), 81–112.

Haycock, K. (1998). Good teaching matters . . . a lot. *Thinking K–16, 3*(2). Accessed at www.edtrust .org/dc/press-room/press-release/education-trust-report-good-teaching-mattersa-lot on June 6, 2009.

Henderson, A. T., & Mapp, K. L. (2002). *A new wave of evidence: The impact of school, family, and community connections on student achievement* (Annual Synthesis 2002). Austin, TX: National Center for Family and Community Connections with Schools. Accessed at www .sedl.org/connections/resources/evidence.pdf on August 3, 2009.

Hill, P. T., Foster, G. E., & Gendler, T. (1990). *High schools with character.* Santa Monica, CA: RAND.

Hobby, R. (2004). *A culture for learning: An investigation into the values and beliefs associated with effective schools.* London: Hay Group Education.

Holloway, S. D. (1988). Concepts of ability and effort in Japan and the United States. *Review of Educational Research, 58*(3), 327–345.

Hoover-Dempsey, K. V., Bassler, O. C., & Brissie, J. S. (1987). High expectations for success. *American Educational Research Journal, 24*(3), 417–443.

Horner, R. H., Sugai, G., & Horner, H. F. (2000). A schoolwide approach to student discipline. *School Administrator, 57*(2), 20–23.

Hoy, W. K., Tarter, C. J., & Hoy, A. W. (2006). Academic optimism of schools: A force for student achievement. *American Educational Research Journal, 43*(3), 425–446.

Hug, B., Krajcik, J. S., & Marx, R. W. (2005). Using innovative learning technologies to promote learning and engagement in an urban science classroom. *Urban Education, 40*(4), 446–472.

Hutchins, R. M. (1956). *The democratic dilemma: Freedom, education, and the fund: Essays and addresses, 1945–1956.* New York: Meridian Books.

Jefferson, T. (1899). To William C. Jarvis (September 28, 1820). In P. L. Ford (Ed.), *The writings of Thomas Jefferson* (Vol. 10, pp. 160–161). New York: G. P. Putnam & Sons.

Jenkins, J. M., Louis, K. S., Walberg, H. J., & Keefe, J. W. (Eds.). (1994). *World class schools: An evolving concept.* Reston, VA: National Association of Secondary School Principals.

Jeynes, W. H. (2005). A meta-analysis of the relation of parental involvement to urban elementary school student academic achievement. *Urban Education, 40*(3), 237–269.

Jeynes, W. H. (2007). The relationship between parental involvement and urban secondary school student academic achievement. *Urban Education, 42*(1), 82–110.

Kainz, K., & Vernon-Feagans, L. (2007). The ecology of early reading development for children in poverty. *Elementary School Journal, 107*(5), 407–427.

Keesor, C. (2005). Administrative visibility and its effect on classroom behavior. *NAASP Bulletin, 89*(643), 64–73.

Kenkel, S., Hoelscher, S., & West, T. (2006). Leading adolescents to mastery. *Educational Leadership, 63*(7), 33–37.

Kerr, K., Marsh, J., Ikemoto, G. S., Darilek, H., & Barney, H. (2006). Strategies to promote data use for instructional improvement: Actions, outcomes, and lessons from three urban districts. *American Journal of Education, 112*(4), 496–520.

Knight, J. (2007). *Instructional coaching: A partnership approach to improving instruction.* Thousand Oaks, CA: Corwin Press.

Knitzer, J., & Lefkowitz, J. (2006). *Pathways to early school success: Helping the most vulnerable infants, toddlers and their families.* New York: National Center for Children in Poverty.

Kouzes, J. M., & Posner, B. Z. (1987). *The leadership challenge: How to get extraordinary things done in organizations.* San Francisco: Jossey-Bass.

Lachat, M. A., & Smith, S. (2005). Practices that support data use in urban high schools. *Journal of Education for Students Placed At Risk, 10*(3), 333–349.

Lam, L. T. (2004). Test success, family style. *Educational Leadership, 61*(8), 44–47.

Lee, J. S., & Bowen, N. K. (2006). Parent involvement, cultural capital, and the achievement gap among elementary school children. *American Educational Research Journal, 43*(2), 193–218.

Leithwood, K. A., & Montgomery, D. J. (1982). The role of the elementary school principal in program improvement. *Review of Educational Research, 52*(3), 309–339.

Levine, D. U., & Lezotte, L. W. (1990). *Unusually effective schools: A review and analysis of research and practice.* Madison, WI: National Center for Effective Schools Research and Development.

Lezotte, L. W., & McKee, K. M. (2002). *Assembly required: A continuous school improvement system.* Okemos, MI: Effective Schools Products.

Lezotte, L. W., & McKee, K. M. (2004). *Implementation guide for assembly required: A continuous school improvement system.* Okemos, MI: Effective Schools Products.

Lezotte, L. W., & McKee, K. M. (2006). *Stepping up: Leading the charge to improve our schools.* Okemos, MI: Effective Schools Products.

Los Angeles County Office of Education. (2009). *Teacher expectations and student achievement (TESA).* Accessed at www.lacoe.edu/orgs/165/index.cfm?ModuleId=1 on May 17, 2009.

MacNeil, A. J., Prater, D. L., & Busch, S. (2009). The effects of school culture and climate on student achievement. *International Journal of Leadership in Education, 12*(1), 73–84.

Mapp, K. L. (2003). Having their say: Parents describe why and how they are engaged in their children's learning. *School Community Journal, 13*(1), 35–64.

Marks, H. M., & Pinty, S. M. (2003). Principal leadership and school performance: An integration of transformational and instructional leadership. *Education Administration Quarterly, 30*(3), 370–397.

Marzano, R. J. (2003). Using data: Two wrongs and a right. *Educational Leadership, 60*(5), 56–59.

Marzano, R. J. (2004). *Building background knowledge for academic achievement: Research on what works in schools.* Alexandria, VA: Association for Supervision and Curriculum Development.

Marzano, R. J., & Marzano, J. S. (2003). The key to classroom management. *Educational Leadership, 61*(1), 6–13.

Marzano, R. J., & Waters, T. (2009). *District leadership that works: Striking the right balance.* Bloomington, IN: Solution Tree Press.

McCullen, C. (2003). Celebrating differences. *Principal Leadership, 3*(8), 34–36.

McCurry, D. S., & Krewer, J. (2003). Addressing NCLB with an effective schools approach: Parents and students learning after school together with technology. *Journal for Effective Schools, 2*(2), 51–60.

McKenzie, K. B., & Scheurich, J. J. (2004). Equity traps: A useful construct for preparing principals to lead schools that are successful with racially diverse students. *Educational Administration Quarterly, 40*(5), 601–632.

McKenzie, K. B., & Scheurich, J. J. (2008). Teacher resistance to improvement of schools with diverse students. *International Journal of Leadership in Education, 11*(2), 117–133.

McMahon, S., Wernsman, J., & Rose, D. (2009). The relation of classroom environment and school belonging to academic self-efficacy among urban fourth- and fifth-grade students. *Elementary School Journal, 109*(3), 267–281.

McTighe, J., Seif, E., & Wiggins, G. (2004). You can teach for meaning. *Educational Leadership, 62*(1), 26–30.

Mero, D., Hartzman, M., & Boone, E. (2005a). Great expectations: Redefining an urban school. *Principal Leadership, 5*(10), 54–59.

Mero, D., Hartzman, M., & Boone, E. (2005b). Raising expectations, giving hope. *Principal Leadership, 5*(10), 23–27.

MetLife Survey of the American Teacher: Collaborating for Student Success. (2009). Accessed at www.metlife.com/assets/cao/contributions/foundation/american-teacher/MetLife_Teacher on March 25, 2010.

Molineaux, R. (2008). *The informed educator: Alternative time and scheduling practices.* Alexandria, VA: Educational Research Service.

Muijas, D., Harris, A., Chapman, C., Stoll, L., & Russ, J. (2004). Improving schools in socio-economically disadvantaged areas—A review of research evidence. *School Effectiveness and School Improvement, 15*(2), 149–175.

Murphy, J., & Hallinger, P. (1986). The superintendent as instructional leader: Findings from effective school districts. *Journal of Educational Administration, 24*(2), 213–236.

Musti-Rao, S., & Carledge, G. (2007). Delivering what urban readers need. *Educational Leadership, 65*(2), 56–61.

National Center for Effective Schools Research Development. (1982). *A conversation between James Comer and Ronald Edmonds: Fundamentals of effective school improvement.* Madison, WI: Author.

Ou, S. R., & Reynolds, A. J. (2006). Early childhood intervention and educational attainment: Age 22 findings from the Chicago longitudinal study. *Journal of Education for Students Placed At Risk, 11*(2), 143–159.

Perone, V. (Ed.). (1991). *Expanding student assessment.* Alexandria, VA: Association for Supervision and Curriculum Development.

Peters, T. J., & Waterman, R. H., Jr. (1982). *In search of excellence: Lessons from America's best run companies.* Thorndike, ME: G. K. Hall & Co.

Plank, S. B., Bradshaw, C. P., & Young, H. (2009). An application of "broken-windows" and related theories to the study of disorder, fear, and collective efficacy in schools. *American Journal of Education, 115*(2), 227–247.

Popham, W. J. (2008). *Transformative assessment.* Alexandria, VA: Association for Supervision and Curriculum Development.

Public Agenda. (2007). *A mission of the heart: What does it take to transform a school?* New York: Author.

Ramirez, A. Y. (2004). PASSport to success: An examination of a parent education program. *School Community Journal, 4*(2), 131–152.

Ravitch, D. (1985). *The schools we deserve: Reflections on the educational crises of our time.* New York: Basic Books.

Rawls, J. (1999). *A theory of justice.* England: Oxford University Press.

Reason, C. (2010). *Leading a learning organization: The science of working with others.* Bloomington, IN: Solution Tree Press.

Reeves, D. B. (2000). Standards are not enough: Essential transformations for school success. *NASSP Bulletin, 84*(620), 5–19.

Reeves, D. B. (2006). *The learning leader: How to focus school improvement for better results.* Alexandria, VA: Association for Supervision and Curriculum Development.

Rickert, C. (2005). A blueprint for safe and civil schools. *Principal Leadership, 6*(1), 44–49.

Robinson, S., Stempel, A., & McCree, I. (2005). *Gaining traction, gaining ground: How some high schools accelerate learning for struggling students.* Washington, DC: Education Trust.

Rodriguez, L. (2008). Teachers know you can do more—Understanding how school cultures of success affect urban high school students. *Educational Policy, 22*(5), 758–780.

Rosenholtz, S. J. (1991). *Teacher's workplace: The social organization of schools.* New York: Teachers College Press.

Ross, S. M. (2003). Effective schools correlates as indicators of educational improvement: An examination of three urban reform initiatives. *Journal for Effective Schools, 2*(2), 67–81.

Roth, K., & Garnier, H. (2006/2007). What science teaching looks like: An international perspective. *Educational Leadership, 64*(4), 16–23.

Rutter, M., Maughan, B., Mortimore, P., & Outston, J. (1979). *Fifteen thousand hours: Secondary schools and their effects on children.* Cambridge, MA: Harvard University Press.

Sanders, M. G., Allen-Jones, G. L., & Abel, Y. (2002). Involving families and communities in the education of children and youth placed at risk. In S. Stringfield & D. Land (Eds.), *Educating at-risk students* (pp. 171–188). Chicago: National Society for the Study of Education.

Schein, E. (2004). *Organizational culture and leadership* (3rd ed.). San Francisco: Jossey-Bass.

Schlechty, P. C. (2002). *Working on the work.* San Francisco: Jossey-Bass.

Schmoker, M. (2006). *Results now: How we can achieve unprecedented improvements in teaching and learning.* Alexandria, VA: Association for Supervision and Curriculum Development.

Scribner, J. P. (1999). Teacher efficacy and teacher professional learning: Implications for school leaders. *Journal of School Leadership, 9*(3), 209–234.

Sergiovanni, T. (1989). The leadership needed for quality schools. In T. J. Sergiovanni & J. H. Moore (Eds.), *Schooling for tomorrow: Directing reforms to issues that count* (pp. 213–226). Boston: Allyn & Bacon.

Shannon, G. S., & Bylsma, P. (2003). *Nine characteristics of high-performing schools: A research-based resource for school leadership teams to assist with the school improvement process* (2nd ed.). Accessed at https://l12.wa.us/research/pubdocs/NineCharacteristics.pdf on August 4. 2009.

Sheldon, S., & Epstein, J. L. (2002). Improving student behavior and school discipline with family and community involvement. *Education and Urban Society, 35*(1), 4–26.

Sheldon, S. B., & Van Voorhis, F. L. (2004). Partnership programs in U.S. schools: Their development and relationship to family involvement outcomes. *School Effectiveness and School Improvement, 15*(2), 125–148.

Shepard, L. (2000). The role of assessment in a learning culture. *Educational Researcher, 29*(7), 4–14.

Short, P. M., & Short, R. J. (1987). Beyond techniques: Personal and organizational influences on school discipline. *High School Journal, 71*(1), 31–36.

Skiba, R., & Sprague, J. (2008). Safety without suspensions. *Educational Leadership, 66*(1), 38–43.

Slavin, R. E., Madden, N. A., Dolan, L. J., Wasik, B. A., Ross, S., Smith, L., et al. (1996). Success for all: A summary of research. *Journal of Education for Students Placed At Risk, 1*, 41–76.

Smith, J. G. (2006). Parental involvement in education among low-income families: A case study. *School Community Journal, 16*(1), 43–56.

Stallings, J. (1980). Allocated academic learning time revisited, or beyond time on task. *Educational Researcher, 9*(11), 11–16.

Stiggins, R. (2004). New assessment beliefs for a new school mission. *Phi Delta Kappan, 86*(1), 22–27.

Stone, S. I., Engel, M., Nagaoka, J., & Roderick, M. (2005). Getting it the second time around: Student classroom experience in Chicago's summer bridge program. *Teachers College Record, 107*(5), 935–957.

Strahan, D. (2003). Promoting a collaborative professional culture in three elementary schools that have beaten the odds. *Elementary School Journal, 104*(2), 127–146.

Sullo, B. (2007). *Activating the desire to learn.* Alexandria, VA: Association for Supervision and Curriculum Development.

Taylor, B. M., & Pearson, P. D. (2004). Research on learning to read—at school, at home, and in the community. *Elementary School Journal, 105*(2), 16.

Theoharis, G. (2007). Social justice educational leaders and resistance: Toward a theory of social justice leadership. *Educational Administration Quarterly, 43*(2), 221–258.

Tomlinson, C. A. (1999). *The differentiated classroom: Responding to the needs of all learners.* Alexandria, VA: Association for Supervision and Curriculum Development.

Tschannen-Moran, M., Parish, J., & DiPaolo, M. (2006). School climate: The interplay between interpersonal relationships and student achievement. *Journal of School Leadership, 16*(4), 386–415.

Turner, J. R. (2003). *Ensuring what is tested is taught: Curriculum coherence and alignment.* Arlington, VA: Educational Research Service.

Tuss, P., Zimmer, J., & Ho, H. (1995). Causal attributions of underachieving fourth-grade students in China, Japan, and the United States. *Journal of Cross-Cultural Psychology, 26*(4), 408–425.

Tyack, D., & Cuban, L. (1997). *Tinkering toward utopia: A century of public school reform.* Cambridge, MA: Harvard University Press.

United States Department of Education. (2003, October 29). *Internet access soars in schools, but "digital divide" still exists at home for minority and poor students* [Press release]. Accessed at www2.ed.gov/news/pressreleases/2003/10/10292003a.html on August 12, 2009.

United States Department of Education. (2004). *Parental involvement: Title I, part A, non-regulatory guidance*. Washington, DC: Author. Accessed at www2.ed.gov/programs/title1parta/parentinv guid.doc on June 6, 2009.

Wahlstrom, K. (2002). Changing times: Findings from the first longitudinal study of later high school start times. *NASSP Bulletin, 86*(633), 3–21.

Waitley, D. (1993). *The psychology of human motivation*. New York: Simon & Schuster.

Waits, M. J., Campbell, H. E., Gau, R., Jacobs, E., Rex, T., & Hess, R. K. (2006). *Why some schools with Latino children beat the odds and others don't*. Tempe: Morrison Institute for Public Policy, Arizona State University.

Wasik, B. A., Bond, M. A., & Hindman, A. (2002). Educating at-risk preschool and kindergarten children. In S. Stringfield & D. Land, *Educating at-risk students* (pp. 89–110). Chicago: National Society for the Study of Education.

Watson, J., Gemin, B., & Ryan, J. (2008/October). *Keeping pace with K–12 online learning: A review of state-level policy and practice*. Paper presented at the North American Council for Online Learning (NACOL) Virtual School Symposium, Phoenix, AZ. Accessed at www.eschool-news.com/2008/10/29/report-assesses-k-12-online-learning on June 6, 2009.

Weber, B. J., & Omotani, L. M. (1994). The power of believing. *The Executive Educator, 16*(9), 35–38.

Weinstein, R. S., Madison, S. M., & Kuklinski, M. R. (1995). Raising expectations in schooling: Obstacles and opportunities for change. *American Educational Research Journal, 32*(1), 121–159.

Wenglinsky, H. (2005/2006). Technology and achievement: The bottom line. *Educational Leadership, 63*(4), 29–32.

Wiggins, G., & McTighe, J. (1998). *Understanding by design*. Alexandria, VA: Association for Supervision and Curriculum Development.

Ylimaki, R. M., Jacobson, S. L., & Drysdale, L. (2007). Making a difference in challenging high-poverty schools: Successful principals in the USA, England, and Australia. *School Effectiveness and School Improvement, 18*(4), 361–381.

Index

On Common Ground: The Power of Professional Learning Communities

Edited by Richard DuFour, Robert Eaker, and Rebecca DuFour

Examine a colorful cross-section of educators' experiences with PLCs. This collection of insights and stories from practitioners throughout North America highlights the benefits of PLCs and offers unique angles of approach to a variety of school improvement challenges. **BKF180**

Raising the Bar and Closing the Gap: Whatever It Takes

Richard DuFour, Rebecca DuFour, Robert Eaker, and Gayle Karhanek

This sequel to the best-selling *Whatever It Takes: How Professional Learning Communities Respond When Kids Don't Learn* expands on original ideas and presses further with new insights. Foundational concepts combine with real-life examples of schools throughout North America that have gone from traditional cultures to PLCs. **BKF378**

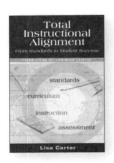

Total Instructional Alignment: From Standards to Student Success

Lisa Carter

Effective education in the new millennium calls for changing an antiquated system. Learn how you can create a flexible, proactive system by focusing on systemic alignment as well as alignment among standards, curriculum, classroom instruction, and assessment. **BKF222**

Harbors of Hope: The Planning for School and Student Success Process

Wayne Hulley and Linda Dier

Create a culture of hope that will improve student achievement and behavior. The proven planning model in this resource will empower you to use the power of purpose to align staff efforts, implement high-yield strategies to enhance student performance, and much more! **BKF181**

Solution Tree | Press
a division of
Solution Tree

Visit solution-tree.com or call 800.733.6786 to order.